Naked Marriage

Uncovering Who You Are And Who You Can Be Together

by
Corey Allan, Ph.D.

Naked Marriage

© Copyright 2016 - Corey Allan, Ph.D.

All rights reserved. No part of this publication may be reproduced, distributed, or transmitted in any form or by any means, including photocopying, recording, or other electronic or mechanical methods, without the prior written permission of the author, except in the case of brief quotations embodied in critical reviews and certain other non-commercial use permitted by copyright law. For permission requests, write to the author at http://simplemarriage.net/contact.

Limit of Liability/Disclaimer of Warranty: While the publisher and author have used their best efforts in preparing this book, they make no representations or warranties with respect to accuracy or completeness of the contents of this book and specifically disclaim any implied warranties of merchantability or fitness for a particular purpose. No warranty may be created or extended by sales representatives or written sales materials. Neither the publisher nor the author shall be liable for any loss of profit or any other commercial damages, including but not limited to special, incidental, consequential, or other damages.

The advice and strategies contained in herein may not be suitable for your situation. This book is not intended as a substitute for therapy or medical advice of physicians. The reader should regularly consult a therapist, psychiatrist, or physician in matters relating to his or her mental or physical health and particularly with respect to any symptoms that may require diagnosis or medial attention.

Names and identifying details have been changed to protect the privacy of individuals.

For information on distribution or for questions contact the author at http://simplemarriage.net/contact.

ISBN 13: 978-0-9973241-2-9

Corey Allan, Ph.D.

To my wife Pam -
I really do enjoy the journey with you

and to Sydney and Will -
you make us look good.

Acknowledgements

You would not have something to hold in your hands without the help of several key people that helped make this book possible. To my editors Blake Atwood, Amy McDonell, and Robin Patchen - you make my words better than they were before. Thank you for helping me find my writing voice.

I must also mention my original co-host on Sexy Marriage Radio, Gina Parris, and current co-host Shannon Ethridge for your willingness to lead the charge with me to help married couples heat up their bedrooms. And Shannon, thanks for the constant push to get something like this on the shelf.

Finally, I'm thankful for my in-laws, Dennis and Phyllis Hogue and their modeling of a grace-filled marriage. Dennis is truly missed and I only wish he was still here to enjoy the journey with his bride. And to my parents, Bill and Joan Allan, thank you for your guidance, influence and willingness to allow me to find my own way. I love you both dearly.

Corey Allan, Ph.D.

Table of Contents

Acknowledgements iv

Foreword vii

1: Marriage isn't supposed to be like this, is it?
But what if it is? 1

2 Myth: My spouse completes me
Truth: You Were Already Complete 11

3 Myth: Happy couples do everything together
Truth: More separation creates desire for togetherness 20

4 Myth: Our marital problems aren't my fault
Truth: Your issues are the marriage's issues 29

5 Myth: My past doesn't predict my future
Truth: My present is a result of my past 40

6 Myth: Maturity equals age
Truth: Maturity is a decision 49

7 Myth: A fight-free marriage is a healthy marriage
Truth: Conflict is an opportunity for growth 59

8 Myth: My spouse wants what I want
Truth: Conflict is bound to happen due to different desires ... 68

9 Myth: Boundaries keep us apart
Truth: Boundaries allow us to get closer than we ever imagined 77

10 Myth: Your spouse is your responsibility
Truth: You are your responsibility 87

11 Myth: My marriage would be better if I just communicated better
Truth: A lack of communication can lead to breakthroughs, not breakups 96

12 Myth: I must work on my marriage
Truth: The marriage works on you 110

13: Myth: Sex is important but not essential
Truth: Sex is essential to marriage 119

14 Truth: You can have a naked marriage 128

Appendix A: Three Surprising Ways to Live a Better Story 130

Appendix B: How to set smart boundaries 138

Appendix C: Six steps toward fully revealing the Authentic You 152

Appendix D: How to Self-Soothe 162

Appendix E: To-dos for great sex for women 166

Appendix F: Three rules for great sex 175

Corey Allan, Ph.D.

Foreword

"You had me at *'Hello!'"

It's one of the most famous lines in cinema history. Since its' debut 20 years ago in the 1996 movie *Jerry McGuire*, it's gotten a lot of mileage. I'm going to give it a little more mileage here, because it's exactly the sentiment I felt when I met Dr. Corey Allan.

I was standing in the exhibit hall at the Opryland Hotel in Nashville at the American Association of Christian Counselor's 2013 World Conference. Corey approached me and introduced himself as a licensed marriage and family therapist, and creator of a podcast called *Sexy Marriage Radio*. Given my 20-year tenure in the field of healthy sexuality, I was intrigued. He and his co-host, Gina, asked if they could forward a link so I could give it a listen sometime.

The next morning I awoke unusually early with an overwhelming feeling of anticipation. Like a scene from *Mary Poppins*, I could sense the winds of change stirring up something magical, but I had no idea what, when, or why. I couldn't return to my slumber, so I began perusing emails on my iPhone. Corey had already forwarded the link, so I decided to just lay there, relax, and soak it in before getting ready to return to the conference.

Within the first two minutes of the show, I was hooked. And a flood of emotion came over me. Here were this man and woman, each married (but not to each other), boldly going where few have gone before – engaging in the most lively conversation about all-things-sexual -- without any guilt, shame, inhibition, or hesitation. I wanted to stand up and CHEER!

But I also noticed another emotion stirring inside me…

Envy. Not the "covetous" kind, but the "courageous" kind. The "Gosh, They Inspire Me!" kind.

I want to do that show!, I concluded within the first five minutes. I want to be a guest on *Sexy Marriage Radio*!

I recalled that Corey had mentioned something about wanting to perhaps interview me about my most recent book, *The Fantasy Fallacy*, so I had no doubt I could connect with them again, and be invited to sow some fruitful seeds into their fertile soil.

Little did I know that God had SO MUCH MORE in mind.

It was Gina who let the cat out of the bag before I even had an opportunity to chase after them with my pitch. "Just so you know," she confided, "Corey is hoping that one or two shows with you could turn into a regular gig. I'm returning to my business coaching practice, so the co-host seat is coming up for grabs."

My heart lept out of my chest. Although I'd had countless opportunities to appear on numerous international media outlets to discuss sexuality, *Sexy Marriage Radio* seemed to offer the one thing that no other TV or radio show could provide -- *Freedom*. Unadulterated freedom to talk about *anything* and *everything*, without anyone standing over the hosts ready to stuff socks in their mouths if they said anything TOO shocking or graphic or socially unacceptable. Heck, even just the word "sex" (or "heck") can be deemed socially unacceptable according to some producers.

But Corey was fearless in his approach with *Sexy Marriage Radio*! He had already been blazing a trail for two years (100 episodes), and I was eager to join him in that endeavor, regardless of how many arrows might wind up in our backs!

Three years and 150 episodes later, I become a bigger Dr. Corey Allan fan with each episode. I feel as if I should be getting CEUs (continuing education credits) with every 30 minute show we record together, because I truly learn so much. And our listeners feel the same way. Each week, we receive dozens of emails, making declarations such as:

- "Since I discovered *Sexy Marriage Radio* on iTunes, I've not been able to stop listening to show after show! It's working wonders for our marriage!"
- "I can't thank you enough for your 'no candy coating' approach to discussing sex within marriage, as well as discussing sex with our own children! These are conversations that we've never been able to have with parents or pastors!"
- "I'd about given up after years of feeling trapped in a relatively sexless marriage, but *Sexy Marriage Radio* has opened up lines of communication, and I'm delighted to declare that our marriage bed is rocking!

We're officially binge listeners because we simply can't get enough of you guys!"

At the time of this publication, *Sexy Marriage Radio* is currently receiving 100,000 downloads per month, and on our 5th Anniversary Celebration in October 2016, we calculated that the show has been downloads over 2.7 million times! Those numbers astound me. You don't create that kind of following by providing a mediocre product, or sounding like everyone else out there on the airwaves. You create that kind of following by bringing something of real substance to the table… something that meets the deeply-felt needs of your audience.

We began hosting our annual Sexy Marriage Radio Get-Aways in 2015, and have been blessed with opportunities to spend four days of face-to-face time with many couples. Doing these live weekend events has revealed even more of Corey's overwhelming passion and unique insights. Each time I hear him speak, whether on-air or on-stage, I have the same thought…

When is Corey ever going to publish all this great stuff in a book???

You are holding the answer to that question. I couldn't be more thrilled that *Naked Marriage* is finally available, because I have absolutely no doubt that these pages are going to rock your world, and ultimately your marriage, the way that Corey's podcast and counseling ministry so often does.

Whether you've been married a few days or a few decades, whether you are looking to enhance an already-strong marriage, or feel like you're dangling by a thread, you're in good hands. Very good hands.

And I believe you'll soon share my sentiment -- when Corey *has YOU at "Hello!"*

~ Shannon Ethridge, M.A.

Life/Relationship Coach, International Speaker, and Author of 20+ books including the million-copy best-selling *Every Woman's Battle* series and *The Sexually Confident Wife*

Naked Marriage

1:
Marriage isn't supposed to be like this, is it?

But what if it is?

Exasperated, Amy released a deep sigh. "How did I get here?"

"You took a left about a block away?" Her friend Brooke's attempt at lightening the moment fell flat.

"You know what I mean." Amy sipped her coffee, unsure of how far back to go. She'd only met Brooke about a year before, but they'd become fast friends. Their weekly coffee shop chats were the highlight of her otherwise monotonous existence.

"How was I supposed to say no to his eyes?" Amy asked.

"Oh, this again."

"Marriage isn't at all like I thought it was going to be. I was so sure when we were dating that he was the man for me. Now, I don't know."

"But you two seem so happy. I mean, I see what you post online, and your life seems fine. Even with what we talk about here, it doesn't seem so bad. Are you two having real problems?"

"No, but I think that's the problem! We're roommates who try not to get in each other's way."

"What about sex?"

Amy flung her hand in the air. "What's sex?"

Brooke flinched nodded. "I see. But you still talk, right? Connect?"

"No, and I miss that so much, but I don't even know how to tell him that I miss it because we never really talk about things that matter anymore."

Brooke focused on her cup for a moment. When she looked up, her eyes had that concerned look Amy had come to recognize. "There's not…how do I put this…?"

"He's not seeing someone, as far as I know. I don't think he'd do that to me."

Brooke reached across the small table and took Amy's hand. "I'm just trying to cover all the bases. I'm not trying to worry you more about your marriage."

"I know. It's just that I don't know what exactly is wrong, but *something* is wrong."

"It's like you kissed Prince Charming, and he became a frog."

"And if he doesn't change, my marriage is going to croak. I mean, marriage isn't supposed to be like this, is it?"

Fifteen Miles Away

"Thank you for taking the time to see me today, Dr. Allan. I know it was short notice, but I'm at my wit's end. I think something's wrong with my wife. She's been distant, sex is non-existent—even on holidays—and whenever I try to initiate, she turns away from me without a word. I've been shot down so many times, I deserve a Purple Heart. I don't think she's seeing someone else, but I know she's not seeing me, if you get what I mean. She sees me all the time, but I get the feeling she'd rather be anywhere else but near me or at our home together. We go to work, come home, silently watch TV, eat a quick meal, then head to our respective corners of the bed. Then we get up and go through the same schedule the next day, and the day after that, and the day after that, and, well, you get the point. I hate to say this, but if I could go back in time and tell my younger self what marriage is really like, I'm not sure I'd paint so rosy a picture. It's not like what my parents enjoy. It's not close to what my church promised. It's nothing like I thought it would be."

Dr. Allan nodded at his newest client, who was sitting on the edge of the couch. "Could you do something for me?"

"Anything."

"Breathe."

I can't fix your marriage, but…

Because we've likely never met, I can't assume too much about you or your marriage, but if you've picked up this book, you may have found yourself nodding in agreement with one or both of the scenarios above. Though fictional, these stories relate many of the hidden opinions that men and women have when it comes to a marriage that has failed to live up to lofty expectations. Sure, they'll share their feelings with a close friend or a paid counselor, but rarely will they share their pain points with the one person with whom they most need to share: *their spouse*.

I'm a Dallas-based Marriage and Family Therapist (MFT) and Licensed Professional Counselor (LPC) with a Ph.D. in Family Therapy. For more than a decade, I've run a successful practice that helps married couples through in-person counseling sessions and online resources, and I've learned something. I don't have the *one key* to unlocking the marriage of your dreams.

In fact, I can promise you that nobody in the world can offer you a single solution to getting the marriage of your dreams. How do I know that? Because the marriage of your dreams is very likely not the marriage of your spouse's dreams.

Instead, this book offers the foundational material I use when counseling my clients. What you hold in your hands is a resource that suggests a thoroughly different way for you to think about your marriage. It's not "Dr. Corey Allan's 7 Quick Tips to Change Your Spouse in a Week," nor is it, "You Only Have to Do This One Thing to Save Your Marriage." Blogs and books that promise specific answers to all of your marital questions serve their purpose, but they can't help you have a better marriage overall, especially as years accrue. Such resources can help you diagnose and treat particular symptoms of a bad marriage, but they can't help you discover a cure.

Before proceeding, you should know that my approach to marriage counseling is thoroughly influenced by my Christian beliefs. I derive my core identity from my beliefs, and my faith influences nearly everything else I believe, including where we humans are in the grand scheme of life and what our relationships should look like. Those core beliefs influence how I counsel my clients, regardless of their own religious backgrounds.

In my counseling practice, I suggest ideas that come from modern psychological research, but I also encourage my clients to consider age-old concepts derived from the Bible. I see relationships through a Christian worldview because that's what makes sense to me. I'm not saying you must agree with my beliefs in order for these concepts to help your marriage, but if you happen to be of another faith background, or if you're of no faith at all, these foundational principles may still change your perspective on marriage and help you discover who you are, so that you can enjoy your marriage like never before.

Now, I'm not promising that a difficult marriage will be cured by the time you finish this book. But I have witnessed many clients who have begun thinking differently about marriage and who have acted upon those new beliefs. Marriages approaching the brink of separation or divorce have found healing. I'll share a few of these stories in real-life case studies I've interspersed throughout the book, although names and details have been changed to respect people's privacy.

The specifics of these illustrations don't matter as much as the issues that sit just beneath the surface of every marriage. You may not immediately identify with a particular issue, but I challenge you to consider how the foundational principle described may affect your marriage. Marital conflict takes an untold number of forms but often finds its roots in very similar seeds.

If marriage is nothing like you thought it would be

I believe a majority of married couples have a false notion of what marriage truly is, and those rose-colored assumptions tend to heighten expectations to such unrealistic levels that these couples often find themselves in predicament's like Amy and Daniel's. Because they don't understand what marriage is and could be, they hide from each other. To keep the peace, they continue the charades, each spouse reluctantly believing, "I guess this is just how it's supposed to be." Consequently, they refuse to get naked with each other in all of that word's scary yet glorious permutations: emotionally, spiritually, and physically. *Naked Marriage* encourages you to find yourself and fully reveal yourself, so your marriage can become fully alive.

Many married people enter into marriage thinking they know what they're signing on for only to discover what they thought are really myths, like "my spouse completes me" or "all fights in marriage are bad." Each of the following chapters considers one major myth and the practical steps you can take to release that myth's stranglehold on your marriage. Every marriage is unique: you may not struggle with certain myths, but I'm willing to bet at least a few of these falsehoods have attached themselves to your marriage.

The unfortunate truth is that all marriages have problems. Size and frequency may vary, but every marriage encounters problems because every marriage involves two very human people. In fact, I believe all marriages are meant to have problems so we might better see ourselves and be matured. From my perspective, marriage is more about two people becoming better humans than it is about two people becoming happy. To that end, let's consider how rediscovering your individuality will help you grow closer to your spouse.

In other words, let's start stripping away the myths we wear like fig leaves to hide who we truly are.

Created to Be Naked

Marriage reveals what you wrestle so hard to keep hidden. But what if marriage is supposed to do exactly that? What if marriage is *supposed* to expose you for who you really are? What if you strip off the myths of marriage so you can clearly see yourself and allow your spouse to really see you too? Isn't that rather enticing—to be truly, deeply, and fully known and loved *for you*?

What if, instead of protecting yourself from your spouse, you leaned into the nakedness of marriage? What if the way we all once were—naked and unashamed—is the way we're supposed to be?

At the dawn of history, the author of the biblical book of Genesis wrote, "Adam and his wife were both naked, and they felt no shame" (Gen. 2:25). Imagine what it would be like to be naked with your spouse, fully exposed and vulnerable, and to feel no shame.

After creating Adam and Eve, God said His creation was "very good," which should lead us to assume that being naked and feeling no shame is a very good thing. Practically speaking, I agree. Not having to worry about what I'm going to wear every day would be great. Emotionally speaking, feeling no shame and being content with who I am would definitely be very good.

When you were born you were perfectly OK with who you were. You experienced no shame because you didn't know what shame was. You also didn't know you were naked.

So why do we wear clothes? Why do we hide who we truly are from the one person we believe who truly wants to know us?

Because we learned the meaning of shame.

Do you know the first thing that happened after Adam and Eve defied God by choosing to eat fruit from the tree of the knowledge of good and evil?

Then the eyes of both of them were opened, and they realized they were naked; so they sewed fig leaves together and made coverings for themselves.

Then the man and his wife heard the sound of the Lord God as he was walking in the garden in the cool of the day, and they hid from the Lord God among the trees of the garden. But the Lord God called to the man, "Where are you?"

[Adam] answered, "I heard you in the garden, and I was afraid because I was naked; so I hid."

And he said, "Who told you that you were naked? Have you eaten from the tree that I commanded you not to eat from?"

The man said, "The woman you put here with me—she gave me some fruit from the tree, and I ate it."

Then the Lord God said to the woman, "What is this you have done?"

The woman said, "The serpent deceived me, and I ate" (Gen. 3:7–13, emphasis added).

Men, here's some free advice: *never* answer any accusation, whether from God or man, with, "The woman you put here with me…" It's not a good idea. That said, there's a more important point to be drawn from this tragicomic exchange between God and his creation. Why would Adam and Eve's illicitly-gained, newfound knowledge suddenly lead to a desire to wear clothing? Because the knowledge they'd acquired signified a deep internal change.

For all its fun in appropriate settings, nudity makes us uncomfortable in almost every area of our lives. Aside from dogs forced to wear ridiculous sweaters, we're the only species that wears clothes. In fact, no culture on the planet walks around completely naked. Even those who wear less clothing than what's acceptable in our culture, like certain tribes deep in the jungles, feel shame when the one string around their waist comes off in public.

We all feel shame when our outer layers reveal what we strive to keep private.

That's as true for our souls as it is for our bodies.

Drop your fig leaves and strip the myths away
Whether you realize it or not, you and your spouse are the modern-day equivalents of Adam and Eve. Ashamed of revealing who you truly are, you've woven and worn emotional fig leaves throughout your life in order to hide your shame. In the following chapters, we'll discuss these *fig leaves* and the shapes they take in your marriage. More importantly, we'll discuss what you can do to strip away these myths that have developed so you can be naked and unashamed within your marriage.

As humans, we're often very adept at hiding who we really are, especially from those closest to us, despite the fact that we desperately want those people to know us and to know us deeply. Why do we suffer from such a subtle, internal tug-of-war when we were created to be emotionally naked in our marriages?

Because of our fear of being naked, we struggle against ourselves, our spouses, and the world at large to get back to being naked, to return to a state where we're content with who we are. I believe that marriage was designed to help grow you into who you're meant to be. It's the only kind of relationship where two different people can learn how to become comfortable being naked with each other. In other words, marriage is the best place to be truly seen and known, which makes marriage simultaneously awesome and terrifying.

In this life, you will never be able to experience physical or emotional nakedness without shame the way Adam and Eve did, but I promise, you can overcome shame a little at a time and grow more comfortable with your own nakedness. Relationships where both spouses can be emotionally naked with each other result in closeness, trust, security, and love, and those are strong, deep, foundational feelings we all secretly want to experience deep within our souls.

That's what marriage is *supposed* to be like, but it takes hard *self*-focused work to get there. Remember: as you grow, so grows the marriage.

So let's get growing.

Corey Allan, Ph.D.

2 Myth:
My spouse completes me

Truth:
You Were Already Complete

After achieving success on his own terms, a good-looking man realizes he's made a grave mistake when it comes to the wife he disregarded, although she still pines for him. He takes a taxi to her house. Within the home and outside of his hearing sit a group of women discussing men and why people don't change.

The man's wife stands up and agrees with the group, "Maybe you're all correct: men are the enemy…but I still love the enemy." The rest of the women erupt in conversation. Then the man walks through the door.

"Hello? Hello. I'm looking for my wife."

The room immediately silences, and the man's wife stares at him in disbelief.

The women cast skeptical glances at one another.

The man realizes he's out of options. "If this is where it has to happen, this is where it has to happen." He points at his wife. "I'm not letting you get rid of me. How about that? This used to be my specialty. I was good in the living room. They send me in there. I'd do it alone. And now I just…"

He sighs and places his hand on his hips.

His wife looks away while every other woman's eyes are transfixed on him.

Breathing deeply and tearing up, he continues. "But tonight, our company had a very big night—a *very* big night."

She smiles.

"But it wasn't complete, because I couldn't share it with you. I couldn't hear your voice. Or laugh about it with you. I miss my—I miss my wife."

In the room, no eye is dry.

"We live in a cynical world—a cynical world. And we work in a business of tough competitors. I love you. You complete me. Not just—"

"Shut up. Just shut up. You had me at hello. You had me at hello."

Marital problems are meant to be

The problem with romantic comedies is that they romanticize too much. "You complete me" is a fantastic movie moment in *Jerry Maguire*, but it's reel-life, not real life.

So many married people buy into to the lie, "Once I find *The One*, I'll be complete." Then one, three, ten, or twenty years later, they realize that the void they thought their spouse would fill is empty, and perhaps it had never really been filled in the first place. They suddenly think, "This isn't working," but they're not sure what "this" is or how to get it working again. It's a frustrating, maddening, defeating place to be. People become disappointed and depressed because they believed the myth that another person was the missing jigsaw piece in the puzzle of their lives.

Those who believe a spouse will complete them are very close to thinking that a spouse will be their primary source of happiness. After all, if he really loves me, a person might think, won't he seek after my happiness within the relationship? That's all well and good until what one person wants doesn't make the other person happy—or vice versa. What should one spouse do if his or her actions fail to make the other spouse happy? Does that mean the love is gone?

If you're looking for happiness, don't look to marriage. Married people who've ever had a conflict with their spouses—in other words, all of them—already know this. Still, spouses tend to look to each other to be the salve to their own emotional wounds. Husbands and wives want their spouses to fill their empty places—holes that were never meant to be filled by anything other than God in the first place. Yes, all of us seek completion, but when we look to our spouses for that, we're asking them to do the impossible.

Now, you would likely never verbalize these feelings, but as the cliché so rightly says, actions speak louder than words. How you treat your spouse (including what you say to them and what you say about them) truly reveals whether or not you're looking to him or her as the main source of your happiness. But happiness can only come from within. Relying on another person for your happiness is like riding an emotional roller coaster when you'd only signed up for the merry-go-round.

Even if you've been guilty of relying on your spouse as the answer to your weaknesses (and we've all been guilty of that), you eventually realize that marriage doesn't fix your flaws. In fact, your spouse reveals your flaws like the clearest mirror in the world. They strip away the fig leaves you've been tightly clinging to for so long. For the most part, you and your spouse don't do this intentionally or vindictively. Reflecting each other—good qualities and bad-- is simply a natural byproduct of living within an intimate, committed relationship where two people spend more time with each other than anyone else. It's almost as if the problems we experience in marriage are meant to be.

In fact, let me boldly declare it: *Marital problems are meant to be.* I believe God expressly created and mandated the institution of marriage so that such a relationship could mature us into better humans. Like an artist finds a statue within a block of marble by chiseling piece-by-piece, so too does marital conflict help reveal our true selves—already complete, yet hidden beneath years and years of history.

The question you may be asking yourself now is, "If I can't ultimately find what I'm looking for within my marriage, what am I supposed to do?"

Well, if I can be blunt, you need to grow up and get naked.

How separateness may prevent separation

Before Heather and Adam came to see me for marriage counseling, Heather emailed me the short history of their past attempts at working on their marriage:

We've been to counselors. We've attended marriage seminars. We've spoken with pastors. We've talked with friends. They all seem to keep saying the same thing: "Try harder. Compromise more. Pray more. Seek more togetherness. Just be better." We tried those things, but if it was supposed to be such good advice, why am I considering separating from my husband?

I remember her email so vividly because she referenced what I often hear from my clients. Like so many whose marriages are in crisis, Heather had tried to put into practice every well-intentioned piece of advice from people in her life whom she trusted, yet nothing seemed to change in her marriage. In other words, Heather was trying to live up to other people's expectations of what kind of spouse she should be. She believed the myth that she had to be the kind of wife others—from her husband to her counselor to her pastor—thought she should be.

Sound familiar?

The cataclysmic change a marriage often needs in order to succeed happens when one person realizes their individuality and chooses to stand up for themselves. The only way a passionate marriage happens is when you are you! Why do you need to be you in your marriage? Aside from the fact that that's who your spouse married, learning to exist as an individual within your marriage is the best choice you can make for its long-term health.

In my practice, I've found the following contrasting illustrations to be helpful in showing how a "me-first" mentality better supports the marriage relationship.

The wrong way to support your spouse: the A-frame marriage

Imagine standing five feet away from your spouse, looking him or her in the eye, and then extending your arms to physically lean on him or her as they do the same to you. Together, the two of you create the letter A as pictured below.

What's wrong with this picture?

In this "A-frame" marriage, where is your focus when it comes to your own stability, importance, value, and balance?

Your focus is wholly on your partner. Your ability to remain upright and functional depends on your spouse propping you up and keeping you balanced. Because of your stance within the relationship, your focus centers on their feelings. If he or she slips, stumbles, moves away, says something you don't like, or chooses to leave you, you'll fall flat on your face.

How does this play out in real life?

A marriage built on an A-frame seems strong—as long as both partners remain stagnant. But life has a way of ensuring we don't remain stagnant. A-frame marriages can quickly fall apart when one spouse changes and the other spouse has been constantly looking to that spouse for their own sense of balance and well-being. If the other spouse isn't there to support them by meeting their every need, the needy spouse falls. In a way, this alludes to the myth of "you complete me." In an A-frame marriage, one spouse absolutely needs the other in order to feel complete. Without their spouse's support, they'll fall.

When that fallen spouse finally sits up, they're likely to react by saying: "Where did *you* go?" or "How could *you* let me down like that?" What they should ask are two basic questions that cut to the core of their true selves: "How did *I* get here?" and "Who am *I*?"

Whether you feel like that fallen spouse or not, this is a good place to begin. Why?

Because those sentences have everything to do with *you* and nothing to do with your spouse.

Standing on your own two feet: The I-frame marriage

How close can two people in an A-frame relationship get to each other? If they're both leaning on each other, they can only get so close as their outstretched arms allow. But what if both people choose to stand on their own two feet in an "I-frame" relationship like this?

How close can they get to each other? As close as humanly possible.

But there are more benefits to an I-frame relationship than just physical fun. Learning how to stand on your own goes to the core of what it means to be an individual within a committed and thriving marriage. This type of differentiation, i.e., maintaining your sense of self within marriage, may seem counterintuitive to what you may have read or learned from your parents or through commonly held beliefs about the oneness of marriage, but learning who you are is integral to establishing and maintaining a healthy and vibrant marriage.

When your focus within your marriage shifts away from your spouse and onto yourself, you will accomplish two goals:

- You release your spouse from the pressure to change (or stay the same) for your benefit.
- You take charge of the only thing you can really control in any relationship: your*self.*

When one spouse no longer has to carry the other's burden (e.g., their expectations, hopes, and desires), beautiful and amazing relationships have room to bloom. When you decide to "show up" in your marriage, take responsibility for yourself, lead your own life with love and integrity, and stand on your own two feet, you and your spouse have an opportunity to experience what you both desire. Your relationship possibilities become limitless.

Move from A to I

How did Heather and Adam fare after learning about the difference between A-frame and I-frame marriages? After recognizing a pattern of carrying more than her fair share of the relationship and not receiving much from her husband in return, Heather moved out for a little while.

She shared that she finally chose that path "when I felt like I could make the decision without an attachment to outcome...without basing it on, 'This is going to change him,' or 'This is going to make him be the husband [I need].' When I got to the place that I could make it because I needed to...that's when I decided to do it."

In other words, Heather opted to stand up on her own two feet *out* of the A-frame relationship. She allowed her husband to make his own decisions about their relationship free of her expectations on him. Consequently—and this often doesn't seem like a rational response—her husband began to engage with her *more*. She reported to me that, even though he'd only skimmed the surface of my marriage course when they'd started it together, when she left, he dove in deep.

Of course, their separation didn't come without its challenges. They both experienced relief in the immediate aftermath because they weren't able to fight with each other as often. But then the relationship deteriorated even more, and her husband, in her words, "really, really detached." This was a make-or-break moment in their marriage. Either her husband would choose to check out of their marriage altogether, or he would be forced to look within himself and ask three necessary questions: "Do I love my wife?" "What can I do to change?" and "Who am I, really?"

Heather was finally able to report a noticeable change in her husband during their separation: "On his breaks at work, he took out the workbook that you put together, and he started learning about anxiety. We both were talking a lot about that and how anxiety is not the worst thing in the world, how it's inevitable, and how to get over it. I think that was a turning point for him."

I've seen countless married couples go through this "new perspective" process to discover both who they are as individuals and how their individuality brings life to their marriages.

But I won't pretend that every troubled marriage ends in reconciliation. By growing up and taking the lead in your intimate relationship, it will either grow and become more than you ever imagined, or it will crumble into dust and be swept away. Either way, the decision to stay or leave becomes a no-brainer. Regardless of the outcome of your marriage, it is *your* job to be a better spouse. Period. And that begins as you do what seems so antithetical to the institution of marriage: focus on yourself.

3 Myth:
Happy couples do everything together

Truth:
More separation creates desire for togetherness

"Stewart, Nicole, do you two think the problems you're currently experiencing are a result of being too far apart from each other or too close together?"

They both give me strange looks that seem to say, "Are you sure you're a licensed therapist?" Then they look at each other. In tandem they answer, "Too far apart."

"What if your issues aren't that at all? What if the reason you *feel* far apart is because you've been way too close for way too long?"

Stewart replies, "I'm not following. We're married. Two become one, right? Aren't we supposed to be close?"

"What I'm talking about requires a perspective shift. Once you see where I'm coming from, you'll begin to understand how much sense it makes. In fact, once you see how a particular kind of closeness works to undermine your marriage, you'll see how you can break out of those patterns and witness a dramatic improvement to your marriage and your own quality of life."

Even then, they still give me that same look, but this time Nicole speaks: "Are you sure you're a licensed therapist?"

Learn to live apart together

Remember what your spouse was like when you first met? Remember how you would look forward to meeting him or her for a date at the end of a long week, back when the two of you were both so busy that the date was the only time you were able to see each other? Remember how purposeful you were with that time? Remember when your spouse's ideas, thoughts, emotions, and reactions surprised and delighted you? Remember when you were attracted to your spouse precisely because of the unique and different way he or she looked at the world?

Over time and in an effort "to become one," one spouse (or both) makes deeply personal sacrifices in order to keep the peace of the household, assuming that that's what their spouse desires. But in that sacrifice, a spouse gives up far more than just a hobby, a friend, or a passion. That person loses an important part of his identity. When that happens, a vacuum forms, and whatever highly defining characteristics are near that vacuum get sucked in. Consequently, a person can quickly find himself being defined by his spouse more than his own unique selfhood.

This is why it's foundationally important to marriage that both partners seek differentiation. In other words, both partners need to learn to live apart together.

Great marriages are the result of two mature grownups with full, satisfying lives who cooperate with each other to get their needs met. In this kind of lovingly independent relationship, each partner complements—but doesn't complete—the other. When you approach your relationship with this attitude, you'll begin to enjoy a marriage where you feel closer together—for the right reasons—and far more attracted to each other.

It's sexy when your spouse can live life independently of you.

Consider the neediest person you've ever known. For this illustration, don't consider your spouse, even though it may be true. What are your feelings toward this person? Are you excited about them and remember fond memories, or is it something different? I suspect it's something different because no one wants to be with someone they feel tremendous pressure to "fix" or "keep healthy." We often have enough to worry about for ourselves. When I'm around needy people, I don't feel needed; I feel trapped. And that's a terrible way to describe a marriage.

A mature, loving relationship should lighten your load, not add to your burden. In order to create this kind of independent relationship, partners have to hold onto their own lives as the relationship evolves.

This is often the point in my counseling sessions where one or both spouses push back: "Are you telling me that we're supposed to live *separate* lives?" I always hear incredulity in their voices. And I can always see greater incredulity in their eyes when I reply, "Exactly." They tend to disbelieve me—or think I'm making some kind of dry joke—because they have often only heard otherwise. Religious and cultural traditions regarding marriage are strong and long-standing, but that doesn't necessarily mean they're right. Often, they're not the healthiest ways to look at marriage, especially when it concerns the dance of individuality and togetherness that a thriving marriage requires.

Living apart together relies on self-care, not self-centeredness. Each spouse should continue living an interesting and fulfilling life *beyond* the intimate relationship with their spouse. Don't misconstrue that statement: it doesn't mean seeking sexual or emotional fulfillment outside of the marriage. Rather, that means that a mature married couple can take responsibility for getting their respective needs met from both their spouse and from other sources (self, friends, family, work, religion, etc.).

Essentially, a spouse looking to defuse a fused relationship should go back to doing what they enjoyed doing *before* they met their spouse. Of course, there are boundaries, but regaining a person's selfhood in light of his relationship is an integral part of breaking an unhealthy fused relationship. It's also very life-giving to the partners who have felt suffocated by the marriage.

The Necessity of Space
Like a healthy human, a healthy marriage needs space. We need space to pursue personal interests and to regroup from anxieties. Fused-relationship marriages suffer from a lack of space, and that can lead to all kinds of issues.

For instance, if you'd like to kill the passion in your marriage, spend as much meaningless time with your spouse as you can. Many married couples I counsel fall into this rut: they spend an inordinate amount of time together when they don't need to, either because one of the spouses is needy or because both believe that's just what you're supposed to do when you're married. This type of coexistence often devolves into a loveless, sexless, boring marriage.

Consider this too: when people don't spend all of their free time with their spouses, they likely won't take their spouses mood swings so personally. They won't default to fix-it mode or mirror mode. Rather, they can have an engaging conversation with their spouses about the deeper reality of those mood swings, helping to dig and root out the real problems. Honest conversation about the surface problem can lead to better conversations about real problems—and that's two mature adults working together to better each other.

The best way to consider why you need ample space in your marriage is to recall life before marriage. Because you weren't together 24/7, you longed to see your boyfriend or girlfriend. Likely, you were both present and passionate because you both knew that your time together was a luxury you couldn't afford to casually dismiss. It's a cliché, but it's true: absence does make the heart grow fonder.

Learning to ask for your own space in marriage and allowing more space for your spouse seems counter-intuitive, but healthy space within marriage is essential. It's also highly important for your sex life, but we'll get to that in the next chapter.

How compelling is the story of your life?
When people make space in their lives for their passions and the people, places, and events that inspire, motivate, and energize them, they're setting the stage for a compelling story. They likely did this without thinking about it before marrying their spouses, but as the mundane tasks of marriage, work, and kids set in, they may begin to feel that the story of their lives is anything but compelling.

What I'm suggesting is that many marriages—post-honeymoon phase—become routine, monotonous, tiresome, and boring. And who wants to stay in a relationship like that? The problem with routine marriages often resides in the fact that one spouse (or both) has yet to discover the story their lives are telling.

When I talk with my clients about this perspective shift on how they view their lives, I ask two questions to help them visualize what I'm saying:

- "If your marriage was a movie, would you go see it?"
- "If your life was a movie, would you go see it?"

Granted, movies exaggerate everything and life can be rather monotonous, but that doesn't mean we have to submit to its monotony and allow our marriages to become rut-stuck stories. To write a great story with our lives, we must first learn what a great story is. You may have never considered how basic great storytelling is, but you know it when you see it.

Robert McKee is a well-known and well-regarded author and teacher whom many consider the go-to guru of storytelling. His epic book *Story* goes into detail about the hundreds of facets of good storytelling, but he summarizes it all with three rules:

1. You must care about the main character.
2. Conflict must occur.
3. A climactic ending must ultimately happen.

Now, these aren't the only rules, but they are the broad guidelines for every story, from Homer's *Odyssey* to today's page-turners. Let's look at each of these rules in regard to how they might apply to the story of your life.

1. You're the main character of your life. Do you care about yourself? Intrinsically, we all do, but as we age, some may begin to care less for themselves. Others may even begin to hate themselves for a tragically wide variety of reasons. When you don't care for yourself well, you will

look to others to fill that need. You'll search for personal fulfillment through your spouse, your children, your job, your accomplishments, or anything else that might validate you, at least for a moment. But this validation never lasts, and when you're alone and quiet and forced to face yourself without external validation, you may be left wondering if you're even worthy of any care at all.

But you're more than just a spouse, parent, or employee. You're a human with intrinsic worth and dignity. You're someone who has dreams, hopes, passions, and aspirations. You may have forgotten what those were, but caring for yourself means listening to those inner longings that drive you to a meaningful life. And as you seek out such a meaningful life, the story of your life can't help but to be compelling to those around you, including, maybe even especially, your spouse.

2. A major part of this book centers on the inevitability of conflict. The fact that you're reading this book likely means that you've experienced plenty of conflict in your marriage. So why would you want to court more conflict? Because it makes for a good story? Partially, yes. But it's more than that. Conflict is a prime seeding area for growth. Conflict is a crucible that burns away the lesser parts of who we are so that we can be the kind of people we truly desire to be.

Consider every movie you've ever seen. The major conflict occurs about halfway through the film, but it's only through resolution of that conflict that the warring parties can ever come to know each other better and deeper. Isn't conflict the central driving force of every romantic comedy? Something always happens to keep the two inevitable lovebirds away from each other. Think about Romeo and Juliet's parentage or *Sleepless in Seattle*'s distance problem. These are external problems in those stories, but they represent the kinds of gridlocked, internal conflict that happens in every marriage. When both parties lean into this conflict, they may fight and argue for a time, but the ultimate reward is a closer, deeper, better relationship when resolution has been achieved.

3. Good stories must end, but there are *many* climactic "endings" to the story of your life. Your end is not your death; rather it's the milestones you achieve in life. Having a child, realizing your dreams, conquering your fears, and learning how to self-soothe, set boundaries, or become less fused are a few of the hundreds of life milestones that ought to be celebrated. When you get that coveted job, finish your degree, start your own company, or take that long-awaited vacation, you should revel in your accomplishment. Furthermore, you should use the confidence that accompanies such climactic endings to start the next chapter of your compelling life story.

If you start to look at your life as a way to tell a better story, you will become more attractive to your spouse. And better stories tend to beget better stories. In *A Million Miles in a Thousand Years: What I Learned While Editing My Life*, Donald Miller summarizes this well: "And once you live a good story, you get a taste for a kind of meaning in life, and you can't go back to being normal; you can't go back to meaningless scenes stitched together by the forgettable thread of wasted time."

He also says that the best way to begin telling a better story with your life is to ask yourself a very simple question: "What if?"

- What if I ran a marathon?
- What if we renewed our marriage vows?
- What if I finally told that secret?

- What if I quit my job?
- What if I started saying how I actually felt?
- What if we adopt a child?

There's no end to the permutations that a simple "What if?" question can take—and that's the point. "What if?" broadens your horizons and shapes dreams into possibilities. "What if?" kicks boredom to the curb in favor of adventure. "What if?" is the key to unlocking your better story. What if you stopped trying to work on your marriage or change your spouse? What if you became more "you?"

To learn more about living a better story, read Appendix A.

4 Myth:
Our marital problems aren't my fault

Truth:
Your issues are the marriage's issues

For the time being, let's agree to quit talking about your spouse. For this chapter, let's discuss your other favorite person: you.

If you believe that the chief problem within your marriage is the person reading this book, then choosing to work on yourself for the betterment of your marriage is a prime solution. Rather than constantly diverting blame for every issues that plagues your relationship onto your spouse, let's take a demanding look within to see why *your* issues might be *the* issues within your marriage.

I don't say that nonchalantly. My clients with marriages in crisis often see their issues as problems to be solved, and their typical answers for fixing the relationship revolve around the *other* spouse needing to change. Rare is the husband or wife who walks through my door and announces, "I need to change, or my marriage is going to end."

In some ways, it's OK to think your spouse needs to change. They very well might. But how much change can you really effect in them? That's their journey and their burden. You actually have very little control over their change—if they even change at all.

Many spouses may not even be aware of the subtle manipulations, covert power moves, passive-aggressive behaviors, and victimized role-playing they enact in order to seek change in their partner. This is what allows us to believe that our marital problems aren't our fault. Even if we're capable of admitting some fault, some part of us tends to believe the problems are our spouse's fault more, as if the percentage of blame for our marital issues are, at best, always 51–49 in favor of ourselves.

I tell my clients who believe this myth that they have three options:

1. Maintain your manipulations (and see how long it takes for your spouse to change).
2. Keep trying to find the magical combination of behaviors that will make your spouse happy (and become bitter in the process).
3. Make your spouse miserable so he or she will leave you (which removes your guilt and blame because they "chose" to leave you).

None of these options is preferable, but can you tell why? Before you answer, refer back to this chapter's first three sentences. Every one of these options focuses wholly and completely on your spouse—and I thought we'd already agreed to not talk about them in this chapter!

Think me-first

It can be very difficult to think "me-first" when it comes to marriage—at least in the way I encourage you to do it. I believe we're intrinsically selfish beings, especially when it comes to our marriages, but we're also masters of disguise. Though we've been led to believe that marriage is primarily about our spouse's happiness, and we often convince ourselves we're working toward that goal, many of our thoughts, feelings, and actions reveal a much deeper truth: we do what we do to get what we want.

This isn't necessarily bad.

What's worse is believing that selfishness doesn't exist and seldom worms its way into our marriages. When people choose to believe that their selfish motivations don't underlie most of what occurs in their marriages, and especially in its most problematic areas, they deceive themselves and fail to serve their spouse with integrity and sincerity. They also continue to cover themselves with fig leaves. So this is where my radically different, "me-first" answer begins.

Being "me-first" in a marriage isn't about placing yourself above your spouse in any way. Rather, being "me-first" means considering how you can change and grow *first*, before ever suggesting to your spouse how they ought to be changing. Being "me-first" also means:

- Showing up, being present, and paying attention to your relationship.
- Considering who you are before digging in to who your spouse is.
- Taking responsibility for your actions and decisions.
- Taking the blame when blame is to be taken—and sometimes even when it isn't!
- Telling the whole truth at all times.
- Setting boundaries and no longer tolerating poor treatment
- Asking for what you want and making your needs a priority in the relationship.

I wasn't kidding when I said this would feel radically different.

When I shared this particular type of "me-first" mentality with a client, he responded, "I'm not sure I could really speak up to my wife and tell her what I really feel. She'd leave me for sure." Ironically, this man had come to see me because *he* was considering leaving his wife! The moral of this short story is that choosing to take responsibility for yourself within your marriage will absolutely come with particular challenges and growing pains. But the rewards far outweigh the risks, and many of my clients have discovered better marriages than they ever thought possible.

The reason this kind of perspective on your marriage tends to help so many is because you were likely "me-first" when you met your spouse—and that's what attracted him or her to you. Let's unpack that.

Though this may be difficult for some, depending on the current state of your marriage, I want you to go back in time to when you first met your spouse. Why were you attracted to him or her? Sure, there may have been an instant physical attraction, but most lasting marriages don't begin from such a surface-level attraction alone. Recall what you learned about your spouse that drew you in. What were the magnetizing characteristics you couldn't help but to be pulled in by?

When you first met your spouse, ideally you were both living fulfilling and interesting lives, pursuing dreams and passions that meant something deeply important to you. (If neither of you were, your relationship was likely *already* in trouble before marriage was even on the table.) Your life prior to meeting your spouse was an integral part of what made you, you, and it was an essential part of what made you attractive to your spouse and vice-versa.

But then a typical, gradual, and barely perceptible shift began to occur. As you spent more and more time with your spouse-to-be, each of you engaged less in the dreams and passions you had previously been pursuing on your own. You may have sacrificed some or all of those pursuits in order to spend more time with your significant other. An unspoken (and maybe even an unnoticed) resentment began to grow.

Why you tire of the one you love
This eventually results in emotional fusion, where one spouse's sense of self relies on the other spouse's perception of him or her. At the beginning of the relationship this fusion is often masked by the idealistic illusion of love, the belief that this is how budding relationships are supposed to work, and then the unending preparations for the wedding. Who wants to talk about deep relational stuff when there's a wedding to plan?

But as you become fused, you become more and more dependent on each other to meet your individual needs. Instead of standing apart together in an I-frame relationship, you begin to lean on each other more and more, creating an A-frame relationship. This leads to at least two major problems.

By that point, neither of you is the same person the other was originally attracted to. Sure, we evolve and change as we age, but we often evolve in our relationships by *giving up our self* rather than growing older. Have you ever wondered how you could initially find a person so interesting, but the more time you spend with him the more you just want to get away from him, either for a time, or maybe forever? The scary question to ask yourself here is, "Did they change—or did I?" The answer is just as scary: *you both changed* into who you thought the other person wanted you to be. But problems have arisen (boredom, annoyance, lack of intimacy, etc.) because the person your spouse wants you to be is *you*—and not the you you think you need to be for them!

Now, because you may have sacrificed deeply meaningful aspects of your life to create a new life with your spouse, a void opens up within you. Like a black hole, this emptiness creates a powerful vacuum that seeks to suck life from the closest human available. In other words, you may begin expecting your spouse to fill the void that was created when you gave up on certain hopes and dreams. This kind of emotional fusion results in neediness, dependency, resentment, and boredom on both sides of the marriage. No one person can ever carry the burden of another person's hopes, dreams, and expectations. They will eventually break from the weight of it. Plus, when you realize that your spouse will never fill that void, you begin to blame them for not meeting your needs. This can lead to all kinds of (vain) attempts at changing the other person.

To summarize, a fused relationship occurs when either spouse (or both) changes to try to become the spouse the other person desires. Consequently, that changed spouse loses their formerly solid idea of self. Because they may have given up what used to be vitally important to them, a void opens up within them that they expect to be filled by their new spouse. When this spouse fails to fill that void, the blame game begins. This game typically ends in one of two ways: one spouse walks away from the marriage, or the spouses seek counseling.

For a better understanding of what a fused relationship looks like in the real world, let's peek into a counseling session with Kim and Aaron.

What does emotional fusion look like?

Aaron and Kim had been married for eight years when they first came to see me. They suffered from anxieties typical to parents of two small children, as well as stress from Kim's teaching job and Aaron's ownership of a small business. What finally motivated them to see me was Kim's repeated attempts to get Aaron to control his drinking and be more responsible in letting her know where he was.

With Kim and Aaron both in my office, Kim began the conversation. "I've been down this path before, of never knowing where he is. He doesn't even answer his phone when I call."

I asked, "What do you do when he doesn't answer?"

"I call him again and again. Sometimes, I'll call him up to ten times in a row."

"Do you leave a message?"

"No. He should answer his phone when I call."

I turned to Aaron, who was sitting beside her. He was expressionless as he defended himself. "I don't think I'm an alcoholic. I just have a couple of drinks a day, and then it's only when I'm hanging out at my friend's shop after work. It's not like I go to the bar and get drunk. I almost never get drunk to the point I can't drive."

Kim rolled her eyes. "Well, when you do come home, you never help around the house or help me get the girls ready for bed."

"C'mon, Kim. I always put their laundry away *and* I get them ready for school in the morning when I don't have to be in early."

It didn't take a licensed professional to know that this argument was about to escalate, so I cut in. But before we go forward, let me tell you about Kim's family of origin.

Kim was raised by a single mother who was a high-functioning alcoholic, which means her mom drank to the point of intoxication but was still able to function in the external spheres of her life, like at her job and with her friends. Because of the alcoholism, Kim was often neglected.

Considering her history, Kim was rightly fearful of what her husband's alcoholic exploits could mean for the health of their marriage and the welfare of their family. However, she hadn't been concerned with Aaron's drinking while they'd dated and during the early years of their marriage (if she even knew it to be an issue then) because she saw Aaron as a way to escape her own life of barely getting by. Once married, Kim attempted to manage her anxiety by seeking Aaron's comfort and support, both through his actual presence and through the financial security he could provide.

But Aaron felt overwhelmed by life's stressors and her expectations, even though she likely had never directly voiced her expectations. Consequently, he would drown his feelings, avoid his wife and family, and relieve his anxieties by choosing to drink with his friends on a consistent basis.

Here's how I helped them see their problem from a new perspective. I asked, "Kim, do you believe that Aaron knows how you feel about his drinking?"

"Yes."

"Yet you repeatedly remind him?"

"Well, he hasn't quit, so…."

"Is he the type of guy who forgets his wife's thoughts and wishes?"

"No, he's actually a really resourceful guy who can juggle a lot at a time and get the job done right."

"So what would happen if you were to let him make his own choices and freely decide how he wants to handle his stress?"

"I don't know. That's what scares me."

"Seems to me that he's attempting to do just that: be someone who determines his own path and makes his own choices."

At this point, Aaron became interested in the conversation. I continued talking to Kim.

"What if his not answering your repeated and panicked calls is actually just his way of covertly asking you to back off? And let's not act like this is a good way to make this request, but it makes sense from where I sit."

My words hung in the air as I saw Kim and Aaron beginning to understand what I was suggesting.

Had I been able to peer into Kim's mind at this moment, I'm fairly certain I would have seen an ancient memory replaying itself, some long-forgotten moment when Kim slammed the door in her drunken mother's face just to get away from her constant harping. Kim was realizing that Aaron was acting like she once did (and still did) with her own mom. All along, she had been attempting to control Aaron's behavior by "mothering" him just like her mother had "cared" for her.

Had I looked into Aaron's mind at that moment, I hope I would have seen a glimmer of a light bulb begin to shine as he realized that his drinking wasn't really about drinking or hanging out with his friends. It was about escape.

As the bulb brightened, Aaron began to understand that he must finally choose to grow himself up or face a life without the people he loved most. He realized he was stuck between two worlds: family man and former single guy. The guys at the shop were all single, and they drank when they got together. He didn't actually like to drink much, but he wanted to maintain friendships with those guys. Like a deer on a lonely highway at midnight facing an oncoming semi, Aaron was faced with a choice, but which way would he go?

Kim broke the silence. "So what about the times when he chooses to go drinking rather than come straight home to us?"

I replied, "What about them?"

"I get that he likes hanging out with his friends, but I want him to choose us sometimes."

"Have you ever said that to him?"

Kim paused. "No."

I smiled. "You just did. Only now you're in a better position to see how he responds. If he's as smart as you say he is, he knows exactly what lies ahead of him."

Aaron spoke up, cautiously. "Does this mean I can do whatever I want?"

Kim stifled a laugh. "How is that different than what you've been doing?"

"I guess it's not."

I spoke into the awkwardness. "The only difference now is that both of you have a clearer picture of what's happening between you two and how your decisions and actions actually communicate better than the words you say to each other."

In the end, the deer went the way of his family.

As Kim gave Aaron room to decide for himself how he wanted to handle his stress, he began to stand up more to his buddies. Either he wouldn't drop by as often, or when he did, he'd drink less or not at all. Kim also began to stand up to her mom more and chose to no longer bear her mother's anxiety or indulge her tantrums when the woman felt lonely and abandoned.

In other words, both Kim and Aaron began to stand up for themselves. They both realized that looking within needed to occur before looking at each other. They saw how shouldering their respective responsibilities for what had led to their current troubles could help grow their marriage. But they first had to understand that their marriage problems didn't solely stem from the other spouse's behavior.

While this illustration provides a specific glimpse into one way that emotional fusion can occur, it also provides an excellent example for our next chapter: how your childhood relationship with your parents tends to inevitably lead to conflict in your marriage.

5 Myth:
My past doesn't predict my future

Truth:
My present is a result of my past

If you're familiar with the story of Adam and Eve, you know that things did *not* get better when they had children. Cain eventually murdered his brother, and the first family wasn't alone in their turmoil. The Old Testament is littered with stories of sibling rivalry and deep-seated family issues.

In many ways, what we face today within our relationships isn't so different from what even the earliest people faced. We are all deeply human, which I believe means we've been marked by weaknesses that often turn us inward. Furthermore, the way we relate to each other—and especially in our intimate relationships—has been handed down to us from generation to generation.

Every relationship creates an interdependent group, also known as a system. You and your spouse create your marriage system. Much of your marriage system is a combination of the systems created within both of your families of origin, i.e., your parents or the people who raised you. In general, systems don't like change, and when significant changes threaten a system, *the system* seeks balance.

If you and I spoke about your marriage issues at length, I'd likely discover the deep differences between your family of origin's system and your spouse's. Because each of you want to re-create what you once had, and because the other person has little clue what you once had, you each try to woo (or manipulate) your spouse to your particular system. But your spouse wants his or her *own* system to rule the marriage.

Thus, conflict arises, even over the most asinine issues.

The deck seems stacked against every marriage, as if marriage is more a painful chisel than a soothing balm. Marriage is both, but far too often we believe our marriages are great when nothing's wrong, yet our anxiety rises in proportion to every problem.

But what if the problem at hand isn't the problem of your marriage? What if you or your spouse aren't the actual, underlying problems of your marriage? What if the system of marriage itself is the problem?

In a way, wouldn't that be freeing?

Understanding what I mean requires some time travel.

The past hasn't really passed
As a child, two factors influenced how you learned to relate to others:

1. How often your parents met your needs.
Were your parents adequately attentive to your needs as a child? Were your needs met in a timely and judicious manner? If so, you likely internalized the beliefs that you were important and lovable and that the world-at-large (as modeled by your family) was a safe place. If your parents failed to meet a majority of your needs, you likely internalized the opposite: that you were unimportant and unlovable and that the world was to be feared.

This is a very simplistic rendering of such situations, but the illustrations serve my point. Still, there are no perfect parents, so I believe that none of us *consistently* internalized such positive beliefs about ourselves and the world-at-large.

2. How the emotional part of your brain subconsciously learned about relationships.

The amygdala is a primitive part of your brain responsible for your fight, flight, or freeze response. The amygdala is also where your earliest childhood memories are stored, but they're stored in an emotional state rather than a rational state. In other words, your earliest memories are much more often felt than known.

Still, this part of your brain subconsciously learns about relationships and stores that information, and this emotional data later influences who you're attracted to and how you relate to them. If you've ever wondered why you made a particularly irrational decision when it came to a romantic relationship, you can probably thank your amygdala for that.

These two factors reveal a truth we know but tend to overlook (unless you've seen a counselor): **the health of your marriage is directly related to how your parents loved you**.

Read that again.

Although your parents' modeling of love within their relationship has affected you, that's often not the main determinant of why you chose your spouse and how you relate to your spouse today. You chose your spouse because he or she helped you re-create your earliest love relationships, i.e., your relationship with your parents.

Because of your internalized childhood experiences and subconscious emotional memories, you will always be attracted to people who allow you to use the relationship management skills you developed as a child—because those skills are the ones you know best. You subconsciously look for someone who mirrors the kind of relationship dynamics you experienced within your family of origin, but you often pick the person who's the *least* capable of meeting those same needs.

In other words, you search for someone to fill a round hole in your heart, but you always wind up marrying a square. Understanding and accepting this idea is a crucial part of creating the kind of amazing relationship you deeply desire.

Now, I'm not a therapist who places blame for all of life's woes on our parents or primary caregivers—far from it—but I do believe that understanding our familial history and relational patterns provides deep insight into how we might change ourselves in order to better our relationships. Plus, much of what we carry over from our families is good and healthy.

We must mine the past to discard the coal so we can retrieve the diamonds.

So let's start digging.

How the past still affects your present
Based on your family of origin, you will co-create a marriage relationship that:

1. Causes you to play a familiar relationship role learned in childhood
2. Allows one or both of you to meet your own subconscious needs
3. Protects you from getting too close or too far apart

Let's look at each of these relationship dynamics in detail.

1. You co-create a marriage relationship that causes you to play a familiar role learned in childhood. Let me tell you about the roles my wife and I learned at our respective households while growing up and how those learned patterns led to conflict in our marriage.

My father was a night owl; my mother wasn't. While he would stay up late to grade papers or watch a game, my mother would turn in early and read for a while before going to sleep. Every night I witnessed the same ritual: my mom would glide past my father, kiss him goodnight, then go to bed.

Compare that familiar family-of-origin pattern to my wife's parents when she was a child. Her parents would wait for each other before going to bed. If either parent had a project or hobby to finish on a particular night, the other parent would help, or simply wait, until both parents were ready to turn in for the night. Every night, my wife witnessed the same ritual: both parents went to bed at the same time.

Pause here for a moment and consider the nighttime ritual you most often witnessed as a child between your parents or primary caregivers. Now consider what ritual your in-laws may have had. (It's OK to ask your spouse if you don't know.) Lastly, contrast those two rituals with what you and your spouse both expect when it comes to going to bed. Are you making any connections?

For us, the first few years of our marriage were challenging because both of us came into the marriage with certain expectations when it came to so many different aspects of our marriage—a normal issue, by the way. But it was surprising to discover that something so seemingly innocuous like choosing when to go to bed could become a divisive issue.

Early on, I sought familiarity by maintaining my father's night-owl ways. My wife would try to stay awake only to repeatedly fall asleep on the couch. I'd wake her up to go to bed, but she would have trouble falling back asleep. This frustrated her (and rightly so), and it would engender even more frustration that I wasn't choosing to go to bed when she wanted to go to bed—just like her parents had done.

To me, the most fascinating issue at play in this real-life illustration is that *neither of our desires were right or wrong*. It's not right or wrong to go to bed separately, nor is it right or wrong to go to bed together. When we choose to go to sleep was something we both learned while growing up, but even this neutral issue created conflict in our marriage.

Conflict is inevitable because family of origins differ, and what we learn early in life often has a subtle yet deep bearing on how we handle our present-day relationships, and especially our marriages. Once you begin to see how your past influences your present, you can prepare your marriage for a better tomorrow.

2. You co-create a marriage relationship that allows one or both of you to meet your own subconscious needs. My wife and I married in our early twenties without the benefit of having lived away from our families or truly experiencing the world as single adults. While there's nothing wrong with marrying young, our relational naïveté led to deep issues revealing themselves early on. Like many young marrieds, we expected a continuation of our infatuation with each other. We believed wedded bliss was surely on our horizon.

But as the early years of our marriage rolled on, that horizon kept receding into the distance. I began to realize that I would seek her out when I wanted something, but I'd push her away when *she* wanted something from me. In other words, I wanted her when I wanted either my emotional or physical needs met, but I didn't really want to meet her needs. Years later I'd realize that this was how my parents often treated me as child. I was re-creating their relationship with me because that's what I knew and that's what I was most comfortable with, despite the fact that such a relationship dynamic was slowly eroding my marriage.

At the time, I wouldn't have been able to so succinctly describe my selfishness, but one particularly important part of marriage made me aware of how often I wanted my needs met more than I wanted to meet my wife's needs: sex.

Stop me if you've heard this before: our desire for sex greatly differed. I wanted it as often as possible. My wife? Not so much. Even when we tried discussing the problem, she would shut down. She rarely initiated sex and seldom seemed to fully engage when it happened. But looking back, I can't blame her. Sex was always focused on what I wanted.

Sex became a gridlock issue for us, a constant battle in our marriage that both spouses wanted to solve but had no idea how to. The problem with gridlock issues in marriage is that *no amount of discussion or compromise will solve the problem.* Why? Because discussion provides a Band-Aid to patients who need a cure.

Frank discussions and healthy compromise have their place within marriage, but spouses in gridlock jump on conversational merry-go-rounds until they're sick of hearing each other talk. They walk away disgusted, and the more often they have to talk through these issues with each other, the higher their anxiety will typically rise the next time they have to get on that merry-go-round. These talks often just reinforce the status quo within the marriage.

3. You co-create a marriage relationship that protects you from getting too close or too far apart. When you move out of your family home for whatever reason—college or marriage or simply because it's time—you don't emotionally leave. In other words, your emotional attachment to your family of origin will never leave you. Consequently (and subconsciously), you will search for a partner at your same level of emotional growth in order to re-create the types of relationship patterns you experienced with your family of origin.

I was in fourth grade when my family moved to a different state because my father accepted a job as a professor in Kansas. Due to financial changes associated with the move, my mom found a full-time job to help keep us afloat. Both of my parents worked during my childhood, and this took them out of the house for long periods of time. With an older sister whose school schedule was drastically different than mine, I became a latchkey kid during my upper elementary, junior, and senior high school years.

Every morning, my parents and sister left the house at least an hour before my school day began. Every evening, I'd come home a couple of hours before anyone else. During this time, porn entered my world—that was far too much time for an adolescent boy to be left unsupervised. Thankfully, this was before the Internet and smartphones, so at least finding porn was a little more daunting of a task.

But bigger than the porn issue was another: this is when my world of loneliness began. While there were aspects of being a latchkey kid that helped shape my independence and creativity, there were also aspects that left me feeling alone and isolated, something I can still feel today.

My wife, on the other hand, was the baby of her family and was raised with all of her immediate family, as well as most of her extended family, surrounding her. She could leave school at lunchtime and head either to her own house or to her grandmother's house.

In our marriage now, we can still see tensions between our two former worlds. A week after we married, we moved four-hundred miles away for my first ministry job, and while I loved the distance from immediate family this provided, she didn't. Her desire to see and spend time with family was, and still is, higher than mine. We still have regular discussions about how to celebrate holidays now that we have kids.

I've also noticed that while I often come across as a people person, I am just as likely to isolate or push people away, and especially those I care about most when they're too close or may know too much about me. I desperately want to know that people care about me and love me, yet I still fight against relationships and act like I don't want to get involved in people's lives. In other words, I still try to recreate a latchkey environment for myself. Yet I am adamant that neither of my children will experience leaving or coming home to an empty house!

While there are pluses and minuses to how your childhood experiences have shaped you, you have likely also re-created aspects of an environment which make you feel comfortable, yet at the same time perpetuate what you've tried to escape. These personal, perpetual issues push their way into your marriage, resulting in the high probability of perpetual problems in your relationship with your spouse.

6 Myth: Maturity equals age

Truth: Maturity is a decision

Marriage researcher John Gottman offers a sobering statistic: 63 percent of issues most commonly faced in marriages *never* go away. The problems aren't the problem though; the problem is the system of marriage itself. Don't misunderstand me. Marriage is absolutely worthwhile. I believe it's even holy. But the system of marriage presents a problem to us because we are intrinsically selfish and immature. I believe God designed marriage to grow us into better versions of ourselves, but that kind of deep, soul-level growth requires being challenged by someone outside of ourselves.

So if most of the problems within our marriages aren't going away anytime soon, what's our recourse?

You can end your current relationship and seek a new partner, hoping that he or she will be able to fill the emotional void that your former partner couldn't. Before choosing this route, you should know that you carry relational patterns from one relationship to the next. You will either find the same kind of person as you did before, or you will find its extreme opposite. Either way, there's one glaring problem with such a plan due to the one common denominator between your former marriage and your new marriage: you.

Or you can choose to grow yourself.

I thought I was an adult when I married my wife, I had to grow up with regard to the sexual issues we faced early in our marriage. It was easier for my wife to say, "I don't like sex" than it was for her to admit, "I don't like sex with you. I get very little pleasure out of it." She had to graduate from a generalized excuse to sharing something much deeper and hurtful to me. Because she didn't necessarily want to hurt me, she chose to share the easier feeling rather than risk increasing our shared anxiety about our marriage.

But tolerating such anxiety is necessary for growth to occur. Though it can be painful, emotional gridlock—where both spouses seek to maintain the status quo—can be comfortable because there are no moving parts. Each party believes, "I know where you stand on the issue and you know where I stand." But things start getting quite uncomfortable when one person chooses to grow themselves up.

For us, my wife started making her needs and wants in the bedroom known. She also chose to grow herself up by viewing herself less as a sexual object (an issue that my past struggle with pornography certainly didn't help) and more as a sexual being. In addition to making her sexual needs known to me, she developed the ability to speak up for her needs and wants in other areas of her life. (It's amazing how much change can happen when a person decides to grow themselves up in one particular aspect of his or her life.) She also had to face one of the most challenging fears of every marriage: the possibility of emotional betrayal.

When my wife began speaking to me about what she wanted during sex, this forced me to face my own fears of inadequacy. I had to own up to my selfishness and unrealistic view of sex. Even more challenging, I recognized a deep fear of being unable to satisfy her sexual desires.

More often than not, I'd always focused on my performance rather than connecting with my wife during sex. Emotion had little to do with our encounters.

As we both chose to grow ourselves up in regard to our sex life, our marriage changed for the better. This change required intensely looking within rather than intensely scrutinizing each other. Breaking free from gridlock issues doesn't mean that you chisel away at your spouse until they break free. It means doing the much more difficult work of chiseling away at yourself.

Before you can witness change in your marriage, you have to choose to change yourself.

How to spot a mature adult
I learned the hard way that age has nothing to do with being mature. I define a mature adult as one who:

- Does what feels right to them
- Lives and acts according to their values and integrity
- Takes full responsibility for getting their needs met
- Takes accountability for their actions, feelings, choices, and life circumstances.

In other words, mature adults recognize that they are a volunteer—not a victim—in all situations.

Re-read the list above. Are you a mature adult?

If we're honest with ourselves (and I eventually see a lot of honesty in my counseling practice), most of us *aren't* doing what we want or taking responsibility for getting our needs met. In fact, many of us have subconsciously reverted back to childhood: we look to others to grant us permission to do certain things or to approve of our actions. This results in grown adults (but not *grown-up* adults) living in a constant state of either passive-aggressive behavior or self-destructive rebellion, both of which are manipulative ways to gain control over what these people should already be controlling—their own lives. They wear a victim mentality that assures themselves that everyone else is the problem. Immature adults tend to believe, "If only *they* would change, then my marriage would be better."

That's relational myopia at its worst.

Growing up within a relationship demands:

- Maintaining a clear sense of self while remaining close (both physically and emotionally) to significant others.
- Regulating your own anxieties
- Not reacting in kind to others' anxieties
- Tolerating discomfort to produce your own growth

Each one of these issues requires focusing on self more than working toward changing your spouse. Learning to confront yourself, validate yourself, and soothe yourself often has a much greater impact on the stability of long-term relationships than better communication and reciprocal validation. (For more on self-soothing, see Appendix A.)

In other words, you must learn how to lessen the expectations you place upon your spouse for your own happiness and validation. In learning how to bring more of yourself to the relational table, so to speak, you won't have to seek acceptance from your spouse. When both spouses learn how to do this, drastic and very encouraging changes can occur in your marriage.

Change yourself and *you will* change your marriage.

Assess your maturity

I believe the four previously cited issues are integral to growing up within a relationship, but many more characteristics also help define whether or not an adult should be considered "grown up" when it comes to their marriage:

Mature Adult	Immature Adult
Honest	Dishonest
Transparent	Opaque / Stoic
Vulnerable	Defensive
Fallible	Perfect
Uncomfortable	People-Pleasing
Humorous	Bitter
Mutually Respectful	Disrespectful
Open Communication	One-Way Communication
Establishes Healthy Boundaries	Knows No Relational Boundaries
Good Same-Sex Friends	Few or No Same-Sex Friends
Lives in Numerous Co-Created Systems	Lives in One or Two Co-Created Systems
Emotionally Stable	Emotionally Erratic
Differentiation and Personal Space	Needy / Dependent
Seeks to meet the needs of self and spouse	Seeks to meet his own needs by excluding everyone else

You may be tempted to look at this list and grade your spouse, but if you've read this far, you should know that that's not the point of this book. Take a second hard look through these characteristics and consider where *you* fall on this list. None of us is a completely mature adults which means that you're likely going to find yourself on both sides of the chart depending on the issue in question. What I want you to gain from this is a framework for how you can begin to grow yourself so that your marriage can begin to change for the better.

But here's the scary part of growing yourself: your marriage might change for the worse. I hate to tell you that, but it's true. Why? Because when you begin to change, your spouse will inevitably begin to change, but whether or not they choose to grow up is entirely dependent upon them. You can't control that. I've witnessed hundreds of clients who've tried to force their spouses to grow up. It never works. Lasting change must begin within.

When your spouse begins to witness real change in your life, they're faced with four choices:

1. They may threaten, pressure, or manipulate you in order to make you change back through events like tantrums, extended arguments, emotional collapses, or threatening divorce or separation.
2. They may submit to you in order to not rock the boat, which leads to withholding and passive-aggressive behavior.
3. They may physically or emotionally withdraw from you because they don't know who you are anymore; they could accomplish this through an affair, living in separate bedrooms, cutting you off emotionally, or becoming overly involved with the kids, work, or hobbies.
4. They may likewise grow up through learning how to confront, validate, and soothe themselves.

If you decide to grow yourself up and your spouse chooses any option but the last one, you will enter into a "crucible" of marriage, a term Dr. David Schnarch coined that refers to severe tests of selfhood and personal integrity that inevitably occur in any long-term, committed relationship. A crucible is a ceramic or metal container used to melt metals under very high temperatures. The benefit of such an intense process is that it can ultimately produce something new and stronger.

A seesaw is a useful illustration for how one spouse's change inevitably causes change in the other spouse. Because you're both part of the marriage, whatever you do will affect your spouse and vice-versa. In making deep changes on your perspective of your marriage, you will upset the balance of what you once had.

If your spouse refuses the changes you're undergoing, you can either hold on to yourself (which requires strong work to keep the seesaw unbalanced), or you can give in to your spouse so that the seesaw comes back into balance (which requires very little work). If you choose to continue your new behaviors, your spouse is then faced with the same decision: assert themselves so that they're on top again, or choose to grow with you so that balance can be reached again.

The illustration breaks down when we begin talking about the ultimate goal of both parties learning to grow themselves up. Seesaws are only fun when moving, but healthy marriages seek balance. So what does this seesaw of choices look like?

How change changes you
When Steve and Michelle met, they were both out of shape. A few years into their marriage, Steve began working out regularly and choosing a healthier diet. Michelle's anxiety

increased as she noticed his newfound passion and dedication to his health. She also couldn't help but to notice that other women were also noticing her husband. Still, she liked her husband's change and knew that she ought to start working out as well, but she missed their dating days, when they'd watch a movie and share Ben & Jerry's. She also began to fear that Steve would no longer find her attractive and leave her for another woman.

So what could Michelle do? She had to change in some way because of Steve's change, but what were her options?

She could choose the passive-aggressive route and say things like, "You're getting too thin," or, "I bought your favorite ice cream today. Let's share some, like old times." She could also be more direct and take Steve on a guilt trip: "You're working out so much. I feel like you're neglecting me." She could totally withdraw and say little to nothing about her anxiety over Steve's fitness infatuation. She could also go into a rage about an unrelated issue.

On the positive side, she could challenge herself to begin taking steps toward getting fit. She could begin to walk a half-mile every morning, then begin cooking healthier meals for the both of them. She could find herself more energized and more secure about her own looks.

Either change Michelle chooses will cause Steve to also change in some way. It's an unending back-and-forth, a tennis match that requires both parties to be nimble and proactive, so they can be smartly responsive to any volley that comes over the net.

What if Michelle begins to court more attention from other guys? Won't this cause Steve to become insecure? What if her newfound commitment to fitness causes Steve to slip into former bad habits? In those instances, Steve then has to make a choice: do I bring her back down to my level, or do I rise to the challenge?

When both spouses keep raising the bar for each other by challenging themselves, the upward growth of each person, as well as the relationship itself, is near limitless. Marriages that are fully alive in this way, where both people seek to bring their mature selves to the relationship, create a strong foundation that can withstand nearly any problem that arises.

It's fascinating to me that even good changes in a relationship can still lead to problems. That's another way of saying that all marriages have problems and these "problems" are the way the marriage works on you. Both partners seeking better health and fitness is a good change, but such changes can still lead to tension in the relationship.

Pause for a moment and consider an issue in your own marriage that may be causing a similar tug-of-war. How have you changed? How did your spouse react to that change? How did you react to their reaction?

Kick Outcomes to the Curb
In the last illustration, what we're really talking about is called first- and second-order changes.

First-order change has a strong attachment to outcome and rarely produces long-term growth because it does nothing to fundamentally alter the system. Second-order change has *no* attachment to outcome and has the most potential to produce long-term growth because it works to change the system.

First-order change tries to solve the present problem. Second-order change tries to understand the root cause of the problem.

First-order change is easy because it's temporary. First-order change is often a default first line of defense for most married couples. Whatever the issue, attempts at first-order change all tend to disguise the same idea: "I don't love you just the way you are. You must change in order for me to love you, so let me help you see how you should change." (If you've been in a relationship with someone who always tried to change you, you know just how bad this feels.)

Going back to Steve and Michelle, Steve might nag, bribe, or threaten Michelle to lose weight. This will probably work, but only for a season, and Michelle will more than likely resent Steve for having made her do something she didn't want to do. But for Steve, this first-order change has reset the balance of the relationship—at least for him.

Second-order change is harder because it's *unpredictable*. Second-order change occurs when there's a fundamental shift within the system. Second-order change happens when Steve sticks to his path towards better health and begins to believe more in himself and his path. With so drastic a change, neither spouse typically knows how the other will react, consequently creating a relationship that may feel even more tense than normal. But let me remind you that second-order change has no attachment to outcome.

This is challenging to put into practice, and even more so when couples in conflict desire second-order change. To that end, let's discuss one of the hallmarks of healthy marriages: how to lean into conflict.

Corey Allan, Ph.D.

7 Myth:
A fight-free marriage is a healthy marriage

Truth:
Conflict is an opportunity for growth

When you and your spouse enter the ring of marriage, you begin the relationship believing that you're on the same side. One of you may be Coach while the other plays Rocky and tries to knock out their dreams. Halfway through the match, you may trade roles, but at least the two of you will always be in the same corner, right?

But as you've read, your family of origin has perhaps set you in the corner directly opposed to your spouse. Conflict in marriage is inevitable, and the more often you hear the bell to start fighting, the more conditioned you are to come out swinging with little thought as to why you're even fighting in the first place.

It's good to remember that no two people fight the same way. In fact, some people's fighting looks like running away. When presented with conflict, men and women face three choices: fight back, fly away, or freeze. And you can tell a lot about a person based on how they respond to conflict.

Men tend to fall into one of two: they fight or they flee. But this often plays out in one way: they fix. For the most part, women tend to fix as well, but some can be fighters. It's the stark differences between Fighters and Fixers that I'd like to delve into.

Fighters are often traditional, patriarchal males in the mold of the Godfather. A Fighter is aggressive, controlling, dominant, angry, and willing to fight, especially when stressed. He's the king of his castle, no questions asked (or even allowed).

Fixers are modern nice guys who want to be nothing like the domineering fathers they may have had. A Fixer is passive-aggressive, subtly manipulative, and freezes or flees when stressed. He also avoids conflict, seeks the approval of others, gives to get, and desires to appear perfect. He's the prince who's never outgrown the shadow of his father.

Compare these general characteristics of Fighters and Fixers:

Fighter	Fixer
Dominates to control	Manipulates to control
Aggressive when stressed	Passive when stressed
Demanding	Avoiding
"Fight" response	"Flee/Freeze" response
Rage	Passive-aggressive
Needs to look powerful	Needs to look perfect
Operates out of fear	Seeks approval/acceptance

Yet for all of their outward differences, the Fighter and the Fixer are very much alike on the inside. They're both trying to manage their anxiety based on methods they learned in childhood. They're big kids in men's bodies trying to get their needs met while creating a comforting environment around them. In other words, Fighters and Fixers are both posers who try to control people and situations outside of themselves in order to manage their own anxiety.

Consequently, Fighters and Fixers see the root cause of their problems as stemming from outside of themselves, which makes them feel helpless and/or fearful to do anything worthwhile in changing the issue for the better. After all, it's the *other* person or circumstance that needs to change. But because of their differences, the Fighter and the Fixer will go about trying to change the other person or circumstances in drastically different ways.

Does it work? Well, if you're in a relationship with either type of person, how often has their fighting or fixing changed you in any noticeable or long-lasting way? The problems they think you have are actually endemic to their own perspectives on life, and until their perspectives change to where they can see their own problems first and take responsibility for themselves by choosing to grow themselves up, the central areas of conflict that your marriage faces will continue to be an open wound until one or both of you choose to seek help *for yourselves*.

Fighters and Fixers don't do well with change. They need beliefs, routines, activities, relationships, and external systems to remain constant so that they can feel safe. Consequently, they're *highly* attached to outcomes and will often work—whether directly or indirectly—to ensure that the outcome they seek is the outcome that eventually occurs. Fighters believe, "What's mine is mine, and I won't let you take it from me." Fixers believe, "You have what I want, and I will try to get you to give it to me without asking you. I may even try to get it from you without you even knowing what I'm doing."

In both instances, the deeper issue is the same: control.

Fighters and fixers are both controlling posers
In the following illustrations, we'll listen in on how a Fighter and a Fixer might respond to the same conflict. In the following story, Kevin is responding as a Fighter. It also helps to know that one of Jennifer's fuzzy lizard-brain memories revolves around her mother shouting at her father and ripping plane tickets in two.

"Kevin, have you made the hotel and flight reservations for our vacation next month?"

"This is the fifth day in a row you've asked me. I told you I would take care of it, so let me take care of it when I can."

"Don't be that way. I'm just excited about our trip. Well, that and you kind of messed up our last trip, remember?"

Kevin rolls his eyes and doesn't respond, sure that Jennifer is about to remind him anyway.

"You called too late, and we had to settle for that room that wasn't facing the ocean."

"I know. I'm sorry. I was busy that week. Can you cut me some slack? I'm not even sure I want to go on this trip if you're just going to keep nagging me from now until then… and probably after then too."

"Why are you being like this, Kevin? You're making me upset."

"That too. Do *you* remember our last trip?"

"What do you mean?"

"You were angry with me about the room fiasco, and it seemed to me you couldn't let that go the entire time we were there. You seemed fine when we were doing stuff, but you seemed steamed when we were alone. Some vacation that was."

"You started it! If you could have gotten the right room at the right time, I would have been in a fantastic mood for the whole trip, but you didn't, and to make matters worse, you never asked me what was wrong."

"Whatever."

To put an even more pointed end to their conversation, Kevin turns on the TV. They don't speak for the next few days. Kevin eventually reserves the plane and the hotel, although their seats aren't together on the plane.

Now, let's listen in to the same conflict, except this time Kevin is responding as a Fixer.

"Kevin, have you made the hotel and flight reservations for our vacation next month?"

"Not yet. I will. Promise."

"Is this going to be like last time?"

"Of course not, honey. I had a lot on my plate then, and I'm sorry that that trip didn't turn out like you wanted. But remember the time before that? When I got us the upgraded room for free? That room was amazing. How about I try to get us a room like that for this trip? It might cost more, but you're worth it."

Jennifer rolls her eyes and doesn't respond to his shtick.

Wary of the silence, Kevin asks, "For dinner tonight, do you want to go that Italian place you like?"

"Sure. I guess so."

Kevin and Jennifer enjoy a mostly quiet dinner, but after they get home, undress, and climb into bed, Kevin begins massaging Jennifer's neck, hoping it will lead to sex. She allows him to massage her for five minutes, then flicks the lights off, turns over, and says, "I ate too much. I'm pretty tired. Good night."

Kevin rolls onto his back, stares at the ceiling, and wonders, "Does she still love me?"

Three weeks later, Jennifer asks, "Kevin, have you made the reservations yet?"

"Yes, but at a different hotel. The one we wanted was all booked for a conference."

"Really? Because I looked at the rooms a few weeks ago and they had dozens available."

Kevin turns red. "I'm sorry, honey. I just... I just didn't get around to doing it until a few days ago. It's my fault."

"I knew this would happen. It's what always happens when I leave you with even the smallest of responsibilities. I mean, it's easy to reserve a hotel room online, right? Anyone can do it... anyone but you apparently. You're just as inept as my dad."

To put an even more pointed end to their conversation, Jennifer slams the door as she exits the room. Later that night, Kevin walks to the bedroom only to discover that the door's locked. He grabs a few blankets and makes a bed for himself on the couch. He stares up at the ceiling and thinks, "I wonder if I can still upgrade our hotel room. Would that make her happy?"

Let's take a closer look at what's going on just beneath the surface of these conversations.

If you've already classified yourself as a Fighter or a Fixer (or you're married to one), you may have a general understanding of these conflict "irresolution" skills. Fighters, as is their nature, are typically forthright. They'll fight, and it's easy to spot a fight.

On the other hand, Fixers fight, but their fighting wears a drastically different disguise. Did you notice how Kevin the Fixer was fighting his wife even though he was trying to give her what she wanted? And can you imagine how deflated he must have been after this experience, believing that he was attempting to do his best *for her* only to be rebuffed at every turn? (Note: the roles within these illustrations could have been swapped. Don't assume that men or women have a monopoly on poor conflict resolution skills.)

Here's the scary thing about Fixers: pushed far enough, they will turn into Fighters, but because they're so unaccustomed to it, they're terrible at it. Consequently, when a Fixer turns into a Fighter, they tend to fight unfairly and strike as deeply and as personally as they can. But as soon as that happens, they experience even greater anxiety than before and revert to their Fixer ways.

So why do these two drastically different types of people desire so much control in their relationships?

Lizard-brain living
Both a Fighter and a Fixer seek to control others in order to not control themselves. I don't mean that they allow themselves to lose control of themselves. Rather, they'd rather have the people around them change than change themselves. That's why so many couples in my office begin our discussions with pointed fingers and "If only you would..." Blind to their own emotional shortcomings and needs within the relationship, they look for external reasons for their marital unhappiness.

In a way, they're not at fault, because they're wired that way. We all are, and it's the lizard brain's fault. The part of the brain known as the amygdala is also called the lizard brain because of its primitive, instinctual nature. The amygdala is the first part of our brain that develops. It has no language capability but rather appears to store emotional memories. Ever wonder why you seem to have more sensory memories (rather than rational) about your early childhood? That's because your amygdala was the main component of your mind storing memories at that time. In other words, your amygdala internalized your early life events at a feeling level.

Consequently, you learned how to respond to conflict at an early age through an emotional lens. If your mother frowned at you or your father yelled at you, your amygdala motivated your response. Again, we can't help but to respond to conflict through fighting, flighting, or freezing. We've done so since childhood.

Here's why this is so important: your primal brain stored that emotional response as a way to try to prevent you from experiencing similar events in the future. When you experience stress, anxiety, change, or other life events that mimic what you experienced as a young child, your amygdala responds in much the same way as it did when you were a few months old. In other words, there are millions of adults acting like children today. It's the reason I'm so intent on helping married couples in crisis learn what it means to grow themselves up in order to grow their marriages. In a way, your emotional operating system has been functioning on outdated software for decades.

Plus, some people may be more influenced by their lizard brains than others depending on the rate at which their lizard brain was triggered before the rest of their brain's development. Even married couples who consider themselves grown up and rational when it comes to conflict have reason to worry: our rational thinking about conflict often arises from our primary emotional memories. We're seldom conscious of our lizard-brain emotions and how they affect us on a day-to-day (or conflict-by-conflict) basis. We tend to believe that our responses are rational and completely related to the situation at hand.

But as a counselor who has listened to thousands of married couples in crisis, I can attest to how ridiculous many of these self-described rationalizations are, and how they cloak the deeper issue of controlling anxiety.

Why do these issues so often reveal themselves in marriage?

Marriage *magnifies* the differences between men and women. Not just gender issues, though, it magnifies our faults, our faux pas, our everythings. When your lizard brain seeks comfort at the expense of your spouse, negative emotions on both sides will abound. In a way, lizard-brain responses to conflict result in an un-virtuous circle where a husband attempts to quell his anxiety by fighting or fleeing a troubling situation, and his wife tries to soothe her own anxiety (over her husband's response) by freezing. In turn, the husband's anger rises, which may cause his wife to flee, which may cause him to fight, which may cause her to fight, which may cause him to freeze, and on and on until either person files for divorce or dies. They can't get themselves off such a nauseating seesaw ride. Until one or both of these lizard-brain-living spouses realize what's occurring and chooses to grow themselves up, their marriage is likely headed for a quick dissolution or a tragic settling for a hard and lifeless relationship.

"But Dr. Allan," you may say, "I can't go back in time and change my lizard brain. How am I supposed to control my emotional response to conflict when it seems I'm already programmed to respond in a certain way? How can I learn to fight right?"

8 Myth:
My spouse wants what I want

Truth:
Conflict is bound to happen due to different desires

Brian and Kate finally get a weekend away from their kids (whom they love dearly, but still need to escape from every few years). On their drive to a secluded mountain cabin, the two freely talk about their hopes and fears, a conversation very unlike their typical discussions. When they reach their destination, they take a long walk around the lake, then head back to their cabin and make dinner together. Brian turns out the lights, lays down a blanket by the fireplace, and lights the fire. Kate brings their small dinner and a bottle of wine over and sits next to Brian. They eat, they drink, and they talk the night away. Eventually, their clothes come off and the room becomes very hot—despite the fact that the fire went out hours ago.

The next morning, Brian smiles to himself over a freshly brewed cup of coffee. Kate winks at him and beckons him back to bed. He quickly complies. Following this second round of intense lovemaking, Brian and Kate spend the rest of their day walking, talking, reading, and simply being. Neither of them have felt more content and relaxed in a very long time. Brian even sees this trip as a possible turning point for their relationship. He can't remember when he's ever seen Kate so happy, and especially when it was just the two of them.

But, as happens to every best vacation, their time away comes to an end.

The following morning, Brian checks his email as soon as he wakes. Worried about the work email he's missed over the last few days and the traffic they'll likely face on the drive home, he wants to quickly catch up and prepare himself for the trip ahead. As Kate and Brian make their way into the kitchen—with Brian's face still glowing from his phone's screen—Brian sidles next to his wife, gently hugging her from behind. She shrugs him off, causing Brian to ask that age-old question, "What's wrong, honey?"

As she walks out of the room, Kate replies with that age-old reply: "Nothing."

Having been married for a decade, Brian knows that "nothing" never means nothing, especially when said while exiting stage left. Against his better judgment, he follows her into the bedroom.

"What's bothering you? We've been having such a great weekend. I don't understand what's going on now. What can I do to help?"

He moves toward her, but she puts her hand up. Frustrated, Kate replies, "If you have to ask, I don't want to talk about it. Can you just leave me alone right now? I just want to take a shower."

Now perplexed and frustrated, Brian provides ample space to his wife and says few words to her as they pack and climb into their car for the hours-long ride back to reality. For the first hour, they both stare straight ahead and let the radio do all the talking. Just as Brian is about to apologize (although he has no idea what for), Kate quietly though forcefully says, "I feel like that thing is more important to you than I am."

"What thing?"

"Your phone."

"What are you talking about?"

"You're always on it checking email, checking scores, checking the weather, checking traffic. 'Just a minute, hon! Just let me check something real fast.' Your 'real fast' is real annoying because it's never fast. You get so lost in that phone that the world around you becomes invisible."

"Tell me how you really feel."

"Don't be sarcastic. I'm trying to tell you why I was upset this morning, and you're making a joke out of it. I can't stand when you do that."

"How can I not make a joke about such a ridiculous claim? You really think that my phone is more important to me than you are? I didn't check my phone for two days! I just did it this morning in case I missed anything and to see what the traffic was going to be like."

"You act like your checking it this morning was a one-time offense. You know it's not. It's an issue for me, so it should be an issue for you."

Unsure of how to respond, Brian stews.

To break the awkward silence, Kate says, "OK, it's not your phone that bothers me. Your phone, it's a symbol, I guess, of how much your work means to you and how much I don't think I mean to you in comparison. I always feel like you want to be anywhere else but with me—unless sex is on the table."

"I'd love sex on the table."

"That's not what I mean and you know it. Can't you just listen to me for once?"

Brian cups his hand around his ear. Kate rolls her eyes but keeps talking.

"I knew this weekend was a fluke."

"What do you mean by that?"

"It wasn't real. It was just, I don't know, a weekend escape from our problems. I kind of wish we hadn't even gone."

"Why is that?"

"Because it makes going back to our real lives feel even worse."

"I don't even know what to say to that, Kate. I thought you were happy."

"I thought I was too. Can you just drive now? I don't want to talk anymore."

"Suits me."

The wrong way to fight

Why is it most of us want to avoid speaking more when a scenario winds up like that? Wouldn't it be better to keep fighting it out so eventually there's a clear winner? Or for both parties to escape from each other in order to minimize the damage? Or for each spouse to comply with the other so the boat isn't rocked?

The answer is to lean hard into the winds of adversity, but what does that really mean? How can married couples learn to lean into conflict so that their marital problems produce sweet growth and connection instead of bitter separation and loneliness?

First, let's discuss the negative ways to approach conflict through the lens of Brian and Kate's vacation story.

1. Assume your spouse desires what you desire.
On the whole, men believe that women want a drama-free, calm, unchanging life because that's what men often desire. In contrast, women may believe that men want change (or are at least mostly OK with change) because change brings excitement and possibility, and that's what women often desire. When these two polar opposite misperceptions collide, an emotional wreck is sure to occur. This basic assumption about your spouse can lead to increasingly greater amounts of frustration within your marriage.

In this case, Brian assumed Kate was happy for the entire weekend, so he was shocked when something as small (to him) as his phone could anger her so much and so quickly. Kate assumed Brian really wanted to know what was bothering her, so she laid it all out for him in hopes that he would change his behavior. Their starting point assumptions ultimately led to a stalling point in their relationship.

2. Refuse to acknowledge or create conflict.
Men are often guiltier of this than are women. Nice-guy, people-pleasing husbands would rather endure hidden, low-level animosity or bitterness toward their wives than speak their truth and experience the consequences. They are not co-captains of the ship of their marriage because they relinquish control so as to not rock the boat. These types of husbands often keep things to themselves, seldom speak, and/or try to please their wives in every way possible in the hopes that conflict will be staved off for as long as possible.

They may also take great (and misguided) pride in their "storybook" marriages. After all, they don't fight with their wives like the other guys they know. When men try to avoid conflict at all costs, it kills the emotional energy (and vulnerability) between a man and a woman, and that's what fuels intimacy and sex.

Brian's silence after hearing that his wife is upset with him is a sure sign of his refusal to lean into conflict. Sure, he gave her the space she requested, but his sarcastic replies to her earnest questions reveal that he truly doesn't want to engage in conflict with her.

3. Eliminate or fix the conflict ASAP.
Again, men are more prone to this than are women, and all too often because men are thinking with the wrong head. If a wife is in a negative mood, a husband will try to swiftly put out the fire. He will do whatever he can to fix her mood and get her back to feeling good, thus maintaining the "possibility of availability." Since most guys don't think a woman will want to have sex if she's in a sour mood, they try to fix everything quickly.

When first presented with Kate's poor mood (especially compared to their previous days of intimacy), Brian follows her and directly asks, "What can I do to help?" He's suddenly lost the woman who had been so enamored with him, and he wants to see that woman reappear.

Consequently, he will do just about anything to make that happen, and he becomes very frustrated when all of his perceived solutions fall on deaf ears. If Brian can't fix or eliminate the conflict, he may act as if it never really happened and hope that Kate fails to bring it up again once they're back home.

How to fight right
There are two major problems in approaching conflict through these means: they don't work and they rob your

marriage of the energy naturally found within it. What's this natural energy?

If the energy of femininity is a flowing river, the energy of masculinity is the riverbank. Masculinity provides a container for femininity's life energy. Femininity feels the safest with masculine consciousness and consistency, and masculinity craves feminine light and energy. That naturally occurring energy (which involves persistent friction, both the good kind and the bad) can be harnessed to grow yourself, and consequently your marriage. The energy of the marriage is what occurs when a man and woman learn how to live with each other "for richer, for poorer, in sickness and in health, till death do they part." It's mysterious and maddening and intense and *foundational* to a long-lasting marriage.

So how can we harness that natural energy when conflict comes?

Bring the Authentic You into conflict.

For the most part, this means choosing *not* to mirror your spouse's mood or react to a troubling situation by way of your lizard brain. For instance, Fighters have a tendency to take things personally when it comes to the heated emotions of their spouses. That's why mild arguments can sometimes escalate into prolonged conflict as each spouse (often unwittingly) mirrors the emotions of the other spouse. If you follow your spouse down emotional rabbit holes, you'll end up further from what you truly want in your marriage. What you want is a relationship with another full-grown, capable, solid human.

To make matters more frustrating, one spouse often will respond to the other spouse's *emotional* logic with their own *rational* logic and vice-versa. So, as the emotional temperature in the room rises, so do frustration levels as each spouse becomes more certain that he or she really isn't being heard.

On the other hand, when either spouse becomes an immediate Fixer in light of conflict, that spouse will likely only exacerbate their partner's mood or, even worse, create a dynamic where the Fixer spouse expects his or her partner to continually soothe and prop them up—the exact opposite of what you want.

Which is all the more reason to bring the Authentic You into your conflict without mirroring your spouse's emotions. For both men and women, one of the best ways to do this is to simply speak up when you hear your spouse begin to react from their lizard brain. For example, when a wife presents a mood that confuses her husband or creates anxiety for him, the husband should speak the truth in love: "I can tell that you're upset, but I don't know why, and your anxiety is rubbing off on me." He may rock the boat, but he's also helping his wife own her Authentic You and become responsible for herself.

Conversely, women shouldn't hesitate to cut their husbands off at the pass if he begins to try to solve their problems. Being willing to say, "I don't want you to fix this for me. I just want you to listen to me," similarly helps men own their Authentic You.

Learning to lean into the conflicts within your marriage takes practice. While I don't recommend instigating fights in order to practice your conflict resolution skills, I do encourage you to work at revealing your Authentic You within your marriage, and especially within your disagreements. This requires confidence in yourself and trust within your marriage, but I firmly believe that such a significant change will help you learn how to argue right within your marriage. To learn how to better reveal your Authentic You, read Appendix C.

The ability to fight with your spouse and still love them at the end of every day relies on establishing and maintaining healthy relational boundaries, something that many married couples struggle to do.

Corey Allan, Ph.D.

9 Myth: Boundaries keep us apart

Truth: Boundaries allow us to get closer than we ever imagined

Boundaries in marriage are invisible, internal, self-defined limits that help people distinguish and separate themselves from their spouses.

Boundaries in marriage are as important as our boundaries for public safety. Without stripes on streets, stop signs on roadways, traffic lights at intersections, and speed limit signs on highways, driving would be a nightmare. In such a state of boundlessness, no one would choose to drive for fear of serious injury. The boundaries on our streets allow us to coexist in close proximity at high rates of speed with comparatively few deadly collisions.

The same can be said of boundaries within marriage: by setting the right boundaries *for yourself*, you can learn to coexist in close proximity at high rates of emotion with relatively few cataclysmic collisions. Without relational boundaries, relationships become selfish free-for-alls where the last person standing wins the right to keep traveling down a lonely road.

"But Dr. Allan, that doesn't make sense. It sounds like you're telling me that building a fence around my heart will ultimately result in a better me and subsequently a better marriage. I thought this book was supposed to help me get closer to my spouse, not push him further away?"

That's a valid question, but there is something counterintuitive about setting relational boundaries. Establishing boundaries doesn't make emotional sense, but I've witnessed hundreds of my clients become emotionally and relationally healthier after learning the importance of proper boundary setting with their marriages. Husbands and wives who once seemed weak and impotent to affect change in their own lives began setting proper boundaries and experienced newfound freedom to act as individual, mature adults within their marriages. Not all of these marital conflicts resulted in reconciliation, but the spouses who endured separation or divorce were able to do so in a healthy manner because of the boundaries they had chosen to set.

Boundaries are necessary because we're all imperfect, which means we can hurt each other, even when we don't mean to. If people were perfect, like Adam and Eve while still in the Garden of Eden, there would be no need for boundaries. We wouldn't feel the need to protect ourselves from others for our own health, because others wouldn't have the power to harm us. Unfortunately, that's not the world we live in, so boundaries are necessary in order to maintain physical, emotional, and relational health.

Because of our inherent imperfections, all marriages are hard work—but some are much harder than others. A married wife in a hard and deteriorating relationship may find herself thinking these questions in sequence:

- Shouldn't he be nicer to me than he is to strangers?
- Shouldn't he treat me better over time, not worse?

- Shouldn't our relationship lighten my load instead of being a burden itself?
- If this marriage is so hard, why did I even agree to it?

This woman may define her marriage as hard, not because of the intrinsic "hardness" of marriage, but because she may be married to an immature and selfish man. (Of course, the roles could be reversed.) But even if this woman is married to a mature and mostly unselfish man, she may still ask herself these questions from time to time. No matter how "good" you are as a person and regardless of how compatible you may be with your spouse, conflict *will* happen. There's no escaping it.

In marriage, the worst in you often plays out, whether you want it to or not. Marriage is where your unrealistic expectations collide with reality, your avoidance behaviors can't be avoided, your attempts at manipulation backfire, your need to please results in becoming a human doormat, your fear of intimacy reveals itself whenever you're in bed, and your unhealthy emotional reactions escalate conflict.

As I reiterate to every one of my clients, marriage is a people-growing machine. In setting boundaries, we play an essential role in whether or not we allow that machine to grow us or to grind us.

The three types of boundaries
The information within this chapter is adapted with permission from Dr. Robert Glover's website, DrGlover.com. Of all of the information about boundaries in relationships, I've found his to be the most direct and helpful in establishing smart, healthy boundaries within marriage.

Internal boundaries allow you to be you. They prevent you from losing yourself in the world or to another person. Internal boundaries are your impulse control, your morals, and your self-discipline. These boundaries can be heard in the small voice within your mind that says, "Are you sure you want to make that choice?" Internal boundaries help you act in a consistent manner while still allowing for flexibility when necessary. With good internal boundaries, you have a strong sense of self.

Many problems I observe in clients stem from a lack of internal boundaries. They get easily distracted and frustrated and choose to do what is easy rather than what is difficult. They procrastinate and have a hard time finishing what they start. They can't be depended upon. They have little discipline, direction, passion, or structure in their personal life. They avoid exercise and self-medicate with food, drugs, and/or alcohol. Many compulsively masturbate and look at porn (or spend countless hours on Social Media). They go where life takes them and accept what people do to them. They have difficulty making decisions, and they have little personal integrity, even while telling themselves and others that they are pretty honest. Those without solid internal boundaries are small ships in a vast ocean constantly being tossed by the churning sea around them.

Internal boundaries can be set by asking yourself the following questions—and honestly answering them!

- What do I want?
- What feels right to me?
- What seems right and how can I act according to my character and integrity?

These questions appear very self-centered, especially within a "two-become-one" marriage, but they're important for an integral reason: **if you can't get *yourself* to do what *you* want, how can you expect to influence anyone else to respect your boundaries?**

Furthermore, people need to understand that setting internal boundaries is essential to acting with integrity and consistency. Rather than limiting you in some way, these boundaries create room in your relationships for trust, safety, and leadership. Imagine what it would do for all of your relationships, including your marriage, if your "yes" was yes and your "no" was no. For men, your wife will feel secure in the relationship to know:

- You always say what you mean, and you carry through on what you commit to.
- She can trust you to keep all of your sexual energy within the relationship.
- You have the self-discipline to exercise, eat right, and save money.
- You won't cave in and take the easy way out, even when challenged.

But if the opposite holds true—if a man's word can't be trusted because his repeated actions betray his best intentions—a wife will likely become guarded or controlling, simply out of self-preservation. In setting the right kind of internal boundaries, a husband can help build trustworthiness into the marriage.

Both genders may need to work on being more assertive when setting and maintaining their internal boundaries. Phrases like:

- "I want to…"
- "I'm going to…"
- "I would like you to…"

are statements of intent, not questions seeking permission. When you stand up for yourself, you don't have to ask for permission, and neither do you need to defend yourself or justify your actions. "Because I want to" can be reason enough to justify yourself, but—and this is crucial to your relationship—be sure to clearly communicate your needs to your spouse in a timely and thoughtful manner while acknowledging that your actions do not occur in a bubble and will affect your spouse in some way. In other words, set strong internal boundaries, but don't be a jerk about them.

Personal boundaries protect you from the world. These boundaries dictate how you let people treat you. Personal boundaries define where each person begins and ends. Think of this as personal space. As an adult, you get to decide who comes into your space, how far in they come, what they get to do while inside, and how long they get to stay there.

When both spouses have proper personal boundaries, this kind of clarity opens up the marriage to true intimacy because both spouses love and respect themselves first, allowing them to bring a whole person into the marriage. This is not a selfish or arrogant love. Rather, it's a love that understands one's own innate value.

Those who lack personal boundaries tolerate all kinds of intolerable behavior. They either try to convince people to not treat them badly or they duck and cover until the storm passes. Life and relationships are exhausting and practically unbearable without good personal boundaries.

Relationship boundaries are how you protect and nurture your close relationships. They are an extension of your personal boundaries. These include the boundaries you create around you and your spouse, such as keeping all sexual energy within the relationship, being kind to each other, expecting that the two of you will work on the marriage, etc. They also include personal boundaries you have with people outside of your marriage that serve to protect the relationship itself.

These are the boundaries that make spouses feel safe and loved, like choosing to not be alone with someone of the opposite sex, or not hiding your friends and activities from your spouse. Proper relationship boundaries tell your spouse, "You are so valuable to me that I strive to protect myself from messing up our marriage by seeking unhealthy relationships outside of our marriage."

Now that you understand the importance of boundary setting and the types of boundaries you ought to be setting for yourself in your marriage, let's consider what a lack of boundaries leads to.

To learn how to set smart boundaries, read Appendix B.

You're Partially to Blame for How You're Treated
As if some of the truths within this book haven't been challenging enough, here's one of the harshest truths about marriage: if your spouse continually treats you badly, you *share* responsibility for that. The worst in your spouse is only truly hurtful when you do not know how to stand up for yourself.

Read that again.

Now consider how that plays out in your marriage.

If you've been tolerating your spouse's physical or emotional unavailability or their hurtful or abusive behavior, it's a fifty-fifty problem, even if you've never retaliated or made mention of the issue. Here's the kicker: you have no control over their fifty percent. But you do have a hundred percent control over your fifty percent. You alone are in charge of your emotions and reactions.

I believe that this is some of the greatest marriage advice no one wants to hear because it requires the suffering spouse to accept personal responsibility for allowing the suffering to continue. If you accept bad behavior from your spouse (or family, or friends, or co-workers), you can likely expect bad behavior in return.

Why? Because you teach people how to treat you.

When you allow yourself to consistently be treated poorly (and cover up that shame with a fig leaf of nonchalance), you're essentially telling your friends and family, "It's OK to treat me that way. I don't mind. I can take it. It's nothing." But deep within you know that's a lie. You may be telling yourself those lies in order to maintain the relationship, but that's a pleaser mentality that will ultimately result in a fused relationship headed for disaster. Even more debilitating are the constant, low-level attacks on your self-worth, ostensibly from the one person to whom you pledged your life.

When your spouse continues to treat you badly, you can be sure that you're:

- Not leading yourself well.
- Not setting proper boundaries in your marriage.
- Unwilling to risk rejection.

Leading yourself, setting boundaries, and understanding that rejection is not the end of your world are three essential aspects of a respectful, reciprocal, nurturing, and mature relationship. If you want a great marriage, you must stop tolerating anything less than loving, respectful behavior from your spouse. You must raise the bar on what you'll tolerate, act accordingly yourself (be what you want to attract), and invite your spouse to follow you there. If you want your marriage to mature and thrive, you must take responsibility for how *you* behave and for what behaviors *you* accept from your spouse.

What spouses without boundaries do
A person without proper boundaries has two options when it comes to their relationships, and both options try to construct fake boundaries bent on keeping people out at all costs:

1. Build thick walls of protection.
These walls can be constructed of all types of materials, like hidden thoughts, addictions, control issues, or self-medication. People who take on too much responsibility (as well as those who take on none at all) can use those characteristics to build walls to keep people out. The same can be said of people who don't ask for what they want and those who seek to maintain an image of perfection.

2. Avoid people.
Avoiding people is easy today, as people can watch TV, surf the Internet, play video games, or get lost in their smartphones and tablets—all under the guise of being connected, but never really connecting with another person at all. Avoidance can also occur through becoming overly involved in your children's lives, your hobbies, and your work. Lastly, avoidance can happen by simply choosing to isolate yourself from the people around you.

We've all been guilty of these behaviors because we learned them as children. If your very first experience of love from your parents was smothering, fusing, neglectful, shaming, abusive, or abandoning, you had *no choice* but to learn defensive boundary setting. Your brain protected your emotions the best way it knew how at the time. Because your imperfect parents (or family of origin) raised you and you didn't have the power to remove yourself from the situation or to set proper boundaries, you were forced to build walls of protection. You had to learn how to avoid troubling situations.

Unfortunately, what your lizard brain stored then still affects you today. As an adult, you subconsciously expect (and even invite) other people to treat you the same way your parents once did. When other people meet that unspoken expectation in your life, you then subconsciously respond in the same protective manner you did as a child. You build a wall or you avoid. This results in an inability to get close to people who have hurt and to truly reveal yourself to those whom you fear or resent.

But there's an altogether better way to approach your marriage. Proper boundary setting explodes thick walls of protection so you can invite your spouse into your life. Healthy boundaries allow your spouse to get close—and stay close—to you. And when closeness happens, fig leaves fall.

But if you're still unconvinced that proper boundaries are necessary for a healthy marriage, read the next chapter's story very closely.

Corey Allan, Ph.D.

10 Myth:
Your spouse is your responsibility

Truth:
You are your responsibility

The following story, reprinted with permission from Edwin H. Friedman, comes from his book *Friedman's Fables*:

A man had given much thought to what he wanted from life. He had experienced various moods and many trials. He had experimented with different ways of living, and he had had his share of successes and failures. At last, he saw clearly where he wanted to go.

The man searched diligently for the right opportunity. Sometimes he came close, only to be pushed away. Often he applied all his strength and imagination, only to find the path hopelessly blocked. And then finally it came. But the opportunity would not wait. It would be made available only for a short time. If it was seen that he was not committed, the opportunity would not come again.

Eager to arrive, the man began the journey. With each step, he wanted to move faster; with each thought of reaching his goal, his heart beat quicker; with each vision of what lay ahead, he found renewed vigor. Strength that had left him since his early youth returned, and desires, all kinds of desires, reawakened from their long-dormant stances.

Hurrying along, he came upon a bridge that crossed through the middle of a town. It had been built high above a river in order to protect it from the floods of spring. Walking across, the man noticed someone coming from the opposite direction. As they moved closer, it seemed as if the other man was coming to greet him. He could see clearly, however, that he did not know the other person, who was dressed similarly but had something tied around his waist.

When they were within hailing distance, the man could see that what the other had about his waist was a rope. It was wrapped around him many times and probably, if extended, would reach a length of 30 feet.

The stranger began to uncurl the rope, and, just as they were coming close, he asked the man, "Pardon me, would you be so kind as to hold the end a moment?" Surprised by this politely phrased but curious request, he agreed without a thought, reached out, and took the end of the rope.

"Thank you," said the stranger, who then added, "Two hands now, and remember, hold tight." As soon as he spoke these words, the stranger jumped off the bridge.

Quickly, the free-falling body hurtled the distance of the rope's length, and from the bridge the man abruptly felt the pull. Instinctively, he held tight and was almost dragged over the side. He managed to brace himself against the edge, however, and after having caught his breath, looked down at the stranger dangling, close to oblivion.

"What are you trying to do?" the man yelled.

"Just hold tight," said the stranger.

This is ridiculous, the man thought, and he began trying to haul the other in. He could not get the leverage, however. It was as if the other person had carefully calculated his weight and the length of the rope so that together they created a counterweight just beyond his strength to bring the other back to safety.

"Why did you do this?" the man called out.

"Remember," said the other, "if you let go, I will be lost."
"But I cannot pull you up," the man cried.
"I am your responsibility," said the other.
"Well, I did not ask for it," the man said.
"If you let go, I am lost," repeated the stranger.

The man looked around for help, but there was no one. How long would he have to wait? Why did this befall him now, just as he was on the verge of true success? He examined the side of the bridge, searching for a place to tie the rope. A protrusion, perhaps, or maybe a hole in the boards. But the railing was unusually uniform in shape, and there were no spaces between the boards. There was no way to get rid of this newfound burden, even temporarily.

"What do you want?" the man asked the other hanging below.

"Just your help," the stranger answered.

"How can I help? I cannot pull you in, and there is no place to tie the rope so that I can go and find someone to help me help you."

"I know that. Just hang on; that will be enough. Tie the rope around your waist; it will be easier." Fearing that his arms could not hold out much longer, he tied the rope around his waist.

"Why did you do this?" he asked again. "Don't you see what you have done? What possible purpose could you have had in mind?"

"Just remember," said the other, "my life is in your hands."

What should he do? If I let go, all my life I will know that I let this man die. If I stay, I risk losing my momentum toward my own long sought-after salvation. Either way this will haunt me forever. With ironic humor he thought to die himself, instantly, to jump off the bridge while still holding on. That would teach this fool. But he wanted to live and to live life fully. What a choice I have to make; how shall I ever decide?

As time went by, still no one came. The critical moment of decision was drawing near. To show his commitment to his own goals, he would have to continue on his journey now. It was already almost too late to arrive in time. But what a terrible choice to have to make.

A new thought occurred to the man. While he could not pull the stranger up solely by his own efforts, if the other would shorten the rope from his end by curling it around his waist again and again, together they could do it. Actually, the other could do it by himself, so long as the man, standing on the bridge, kept it still and steady.

"Now listen," he shouted down. "I think I know how to save you." And he explained his plan.

But the other man wasn't interested.

"You mean you won't help? But I told you I cannot pull you up myself, and I don't think I can hang on much longer either."

"You must try," the stranger shouted back tearfully. "If you fail, I die."

What should he do? His life or the other's? And then, a new idea. A revelation. So new, in fact, it seemed heretical, so alien was it to his traditional way of thinking.

"I want you to listen carefully," the man said, "because I mean what I am about to say. I will not accept the position of choice for your life, only for my own; the position of choice for your own life I hereby give back to you."

"What do you mean?" the other man asked, afraid.

"I mean, simply, it's up to you. You decide which way this ends. I will become the counterweight. You do the pulling and bring yourself up. I will even tug a little from here." He began unwinding the rope from around his waist and braced himself anew against the side.

"You cannot mean what you say!" the stranger shrieked. "You would not be so selfish. I am your responsibility. What could be so important that you would let someone die? Do not do this to me."

The man waited a moment. There was no change in the tension of the rope. "I accept your choice," he said at last, and freed his hands.

Which person are you?

Friedman's striking illustration externally captures the internal worlds of those made prisoners by fused relationships. Tethered to a desperately needy person, one who may even believe that his or her life wholly depends upon someone else, prisoners of fused relationships are ultimately forced to make a "selfish" decision. Yet in choosing to grow themselves up and to not allow themselves to be further dragged down by their partner, these "me-first" mentality spouses begin to learn that a healthy relationship does not, in fact, involve one person dangling off the edge of a bridge.

Once the bridge-jumper likewise recognizes the ridiculousness of the situation into which they've willingly cast themselves, that relationship has a much greater chance of thriving too. When both people are able to live from a place where their feet are on solid ground—without being involuntarily tethered to each other—the path before them presents a much brighter and more open future than it had when they were constantly living in an immobile, life-or-death seesaw match of emotional imprisonment.

As always, the question here isn't necessarily about whether your spouse is a bridge-jumper. You may need to ask yourself, are you?

Why fused relationships so often fail

A majority of the couples I counsel will answer that their marital problems are because they're too far apart. After all, when they sit in my office, that's how they feel. They're there because they need help and feel as if their spouse (or they themselves) is slowly receding from the relationship. But often, what they don't realize is that they're at the endpoint of a much longer journey, one where at least one spouse has been far too dependent on the other. Now, this isn't a description of all marriages, but it is an apt illustration for marriages suffering from emotional fusion.

In fused relationships, there is no "I," only "we." At least one party in a fused relationship expects that his or her spouse should think, behave, believe, and desire as they do. At least one party expects that his or her spouse essentially exists to meet their needs. At least one party wants the other to conform in order to decrease their own anxiety. That needy spouse may not say as much (or even realize what they're doing), but their actions will always reveal their motivations.

Fused relationships kill marriages because they put too heavy a burden on one spouse and grant too little control to the other. A fused person who seeks to have his or her needs filled by their spouse is ultimately releasing control of their lives to another person. The fused person assumes a victimhood mentality, where everything that happens to him or her is the spouse's fault (or at least someone else's). This puts an unmanageable burden on the spouse and creates a prime environment for marital problems to fester.

The codependent spouse chases after the independent spouse in order to have his or her needs met, but the independent spouse runs away because they know they can never meet those needs. As years and years pass, at least one of the spouses is going to tire of the race and choose to drop out altogether.

As in "The Bridge," one spouse essentially takes the other spouse hostage to their own emotions—and neither spouse is having fun or able to truly love the other person well. A fused relationship kills any chances of having an evolving, passionate, fulfilling marriage because the more fused they become, the more they will ultimately resent each other. As resentment builds, vain attempts at changing each other also increase while sexual passion quickly fades away.

The person you once vowed to never leave now seems like the only person you can't escape.

Fused relationships are characterized by:

- Guilt, because you want something different and you know your spouse will not like your independent thinking.
- Unspoken expectations, which are rules or ideals about the relationship that were not discussed with each other.
- Emotional eruptions, because often unspoken expectations have not been met.
- Passive-aggressiveness, as a way for a codependent partner to get what he or she wants without conflict.
- Isolation, in an effort to make the independent party seek out and draw near to the codependent spouse.
- Secrets
- Hidden behaviors
- Rebellion

Fused systems thrive on unrealistic expectations like:

- Because you are my husband, you should always answer the phone when I call.
- Because you are my wife, you should never talk to other men.
- Because you are my husband, you should want to be around me as much as I want to be around you.
- Because you are my wife, you should want to have sex as often as I want.
- Because a clean house is important to me, it should be just as important to you.
- Because I sacrifice so much for you, you should always appreciate me and never get mad at me.

When a codependent person places these kinds of burdens on his or her spouse, the spouse will feel the need to kick back like a horse saddled with too much weight. Independent spouses do this, not because they don't still love their spouses, but because it's often their only recourse to have their own space in the relationships and hold onto themselves in any significant way.

This "kick back" often occurs in the guise of acting out and/or self-destructive behavior by the independent spouse. It's after such behavior that couples often seek counseling. Essentially, the slow simmer of a fused relationship has now boiled over into the marriage. The codependent spouse, who may have thought nothing was *that* wrong with their marriage, has now witnessed that something is *very* wrong with their marriage. But ironically enough, the codependent spouse may only see his or her spouse's detrimental actions and conclude that their marriage problems are all the *the other spouse's* fault. They likely won't become aware of their own shortcomings until a few brutally honest conversations later in my office with them and their spouse.

Much of boundary setting relies on effective, forthright communication between spouses, but what happens when communication breaks down? Is the end drawing near?

11 Myth: My marriage would be better if I just communicated better

Truth: A lack of communication can lead to breakthroughs, not breakups

Ross and Courtney sat silently in their car, inching along the highway. Because of a recent accident, they were sharing one car, and Ross had to take his wife to work. That accident, plus the other issues they'd recently been facing in their marriage, had led to more than one silent drive in recent weeks.

Courtney attempted conversation.

"How's your coffee?"

Ross curtly replied, "Cold," while also thinking "Just like you."

"I'm sorry about that. I should have put it in a better mug."

"Yeah, that would have been nice. It's the only hot thing I have to look forward to these days."

"What is *that* supposed to mean?"

Ross suddenly realized that he'd spoken what he'd only meant to think.

"I didn't mean any—"

"Watch out!"

Ross slammed the brakes, stopping inches from the car in front of him.

"Looks like we're not going anywhere for a while."

They sat in silence for a few minutes, though they both felt like hours passed.

In a calmer voice, Courtney asked, "Ross, will you please tell me what you meant by that?"

"I didn't mean to say that. I'm sorry."

"But you said it, so you were thinking it."

"It's just that we never, you know, do it as much as we used to."

"Do what?"

"*It*."

"Oh, this again."

"What do you mean *this again*?"

"I know you want more sex. We've beat around this bush a hundred times in the last six months."

"I haven't been near a bush in ages and you know it."

"Very funny. Why do we have to talk about this now?"

"You're the one who brought it up! Plus, why do you think I keep bringing it up? It's important to me, but I don't think you really understand that. You just assume I'm just like every other guy and sex is the only reason I'm with you."

"Well, if you could be a little bit more romantic and not just want to immediately dive into sex, that could help."

"Oh, now I'm not romantic? What about that deck I built for you?"

"That's not…oh, never mind. I don't want to argue about this anymore. Just get me to work."

Ross and Courtney returned to silence while the gridlock stretched out for miles before them.

When words fail, your relationship doesn't have to as well
Couples often see gridlock as the beginning of the end. In reality, it's only a midpoint toward your final destination. Getting past gridlock is absolutely necessary for a marriage that lasts.

Gridlock occurs when the spouses are so polarized that they can't consider the other person's perspective, resulting in a state of inertia. This often happens when one or both spouses has begun setting firm boundaries in their lives. Gridlock is inevitable in all close relationships because two people will inevitably disagree about large issues in marriage and parenting.

Dr. David Schnarch said, "All couples eventually hit emotional gridlock when partners are at each other's throats, arguing about everything, and no one can give an inch or say they're sorry." Emotional gridlock happens when each partner defines a position on an issue that blocks his or her spouse's preferred position. Just like gridlock in traffic, emotional gridlock causes everything to come to a maddening standstill.

Your marriage is suffering from emotional gridlock when you find yourself repeatedly having the same arguments. They will likely even have the same triggers and transpire in similar ways. The arguing may become so routine that you and your spouse could switch positions and still have the same argument. At this point, tired and worn down by the repetitive stress and heightened anxiety just waiting for your spouse to say *those* words, many couples feel as if the easiest way out is to just quit the relationship.

But for all of its ills, there are two important factors to remember in regard to emotional gridlock:

1. Gridlock is natural to every committed relationship.
2. Gridlock proves that each spouse is still invested in the relationship.

Conflict is a sign that the two of you still care enough about each other to get upset when you disagree. Of course, the disagreement may be heated and make your blood boil, but if your spouse opts for never fighting, he or she has likely already checked out.

Choose to view gridlock as the means to an end and not an end itself. If you view gridlock as a sure sign of a failed marriage, you'll be much more prone to allowing the normal difficulties of marriage to lead you into an easy divorce. After all, if gridlock is inevitable in marriage and you choose to run from one marriage because of gridlock, guess what you'll find in your next marriage?

Marriage unites two very different people. Conflict and gridlock will happen. The question is, how will you choose to use gridlock to mature yourself and grow your marriage?

How to escape gridlock without escaping your marriage

Because well-meaning friends, religious leaders, and even counselors tend to encourage more communication as the answer to major marital issues, couples locked in gridlock attempt that route. **But communication is neither the cause nor the solution to gridlock.** In fact, more communication will likely make the gridlock even deadlier to the relationship. If you're experiencing such a state, the last thing you want to do is talk about the problem *more*. What you want is a solution.

And, let's be honest: what you really, really want is *your* solution.

Therein lies the problem. You want what you want (and haven't I been telling you, that's what needs to happen?) and your spouse wants what your spouse wants. Yet when the both of you are diametrically opposed to the other with no sign of giving in, emotional gridlock stops the relationship in its tracks. More communication either makes the situation worse, or all communication is haunted by the vast rain cloud of argument that constantly hovers over your heads. The marriage essentially takes a backseat until that one pressing issue is resolved, which is why it's all the more important to learn how to get through gridlock.

Gridlock can happen for nearly any reason, but certain major issues lead to gridlock more than others, and they're all issues you would expect. Sex, intimacy, money, parenting, and in-laws are just a few of the most common problems. Choices *must* be made in regard to these issues, and these choices often have far-ranging and long-lasting implications for you, your spouse, and other people in your life. These choices require a married couple to be on the same page, but what if one spouse can't get on the other spouse's page? What if one spouse refuses to even read the other spouse's page? Gridlock ensues.

To free yourself from a bondage to gridlock:

1. Take responsibility for yourself.
You can't change your spouse. If you're in gridlock right now, you know that to be true. In attempting to manage gridlock on your own and in the hopes of not further upsetting your spouse, you may have become somewhat codependent and overly attached to your spouse. You may have no boundaries, or the boundaries you do have are

unclear and easily transgressed. It's important to deal with those issues before working on getting out of gridlock. You must learn more responsibility for yourself and become less dependent on your spouse in order to see gridlock become nothing more than a frustrating time in your rearview mirror.

When a spouse is overly depends on his or her mate for understanding, sympathy, acceptance, or accommodation, the likelihood for gridlock increases. I'm not saying that you shouldn't look for those healthy experiences from your spouse. Rather, I'm warning you about doing so in an excessive manner. What happens when your spouse fails to meet those needs? What if your spouse isn't even capable of meeting those needs? Or what if your strong desire for those experiences results in making it more difficult for your spouse to meet your needs? If you demand (whether verbally or not) that your needs be met by your spouse—if you turn your needs into ultimatums—gridlock is inevitable.

For example, sex and intimacy go together like two tangled bodies in bed, but as necessary and fun as those experiences are, they can lead to conflict and gridlock within marriage. But like every other issue that results in conflict, you can choose to use those moments to experience a breakthrough rather than a breakup. When you find yourself in emotional gridlock with your spouse, you're actually in the perfect spot to live more in line with your boundaries and become more mature.

If you're gridlocked over exactly what needs to happen in order for you to get what you want (more sex, more intimacy, more help with the kids or housework, more time with extended family, etc.), you're already in trouble. Truth is there is lots to fight about in marriage, and gridlock is likely to happen. To make it through gridlock requires taking more responsibility for yourself and your action. *A marriage fully alive is one where you give without expecting anything in return.* A marker of an emotionally mature human is their ability to give with no strings attached: giving out of fullness rather than emptiness, giving out of choice rather than demands.

And a giving spouse is hard to argue with.

2. Share yourself with your spouse.

The best way to maintain gridlock is to keep demanding your way or complaining about your spouse's inability to come around to your way of thinking. When your arguments keep revolving around these issues, your spouse is very likely to respond with defensiveness, which often leads to him or her feeling pressured to revert to the way things have always been. Consequently, the conflict goes unresolved and gridlock cements itself into the marriage.

Growing through gridlock means choosing to share yourself with your spouse and doing the right thing regardless of your spouse's reaction. You must be able to give affirmation, validation, and trust *without expecting your spouse to respond in kind.* Giving of yourself in this way is risky, frightening, and perilous, but it will also make you a stronger person.

Don't get me wrong: desiring stability, satisfaction, comfort, togetherness, empathy, and love from your marriage is proper and healthy. It's not these desires that get you in trouble. Rather, it's your reaction to your unmet needs (or unrealistic expectations) and the particular strategies you employ when you don't get what you want.

Consider this: when your spouse's negative attitude creeps into your marriage and seeps into your arguments, is it easier to match his or her negativity with your own, or to remain positive and hopeful for the betterment of the relationship? For a vast majority of us, it's easier to respond with negativity. In fact, it's almost an automatic reflex—as if one's lizard brain responds before better thoughts take control. But leaning into conflict means learning to understand your lizard-brain reactions and how *not* to let them control your responses to stressful situations in your marriage. Being mature means holding back your negative emotions.

3. Validate yourself.
You must have a self before being able to give of that self to someone else. In other words, you must learn how to self-validate rather than constantly to seek validation from external sources, namely, your spouse. Self-validation is being OK with yourself regardless of what others say or do. Self-validation is what you believe about yourself unencumbered by others' criticism or evaluation.

The trouble with marriage and self-validation is that far too many of us approach marriage as the greatest validation of who we are. "She picked me!" "He wants to marry me!" In the afterglow of the honeymoon, and before the reality of marriage has had time to fully reveal itself, a married couple may likewise suffer from the delusion that their relationship will play out like a tightly choreographed dance. "I'm sure he already understands what I need." "How could she not know what I want?"

Both of these beliefs—marriage validates me and we'll always be on the same page—perpetuate gridlock.

Traditional vows include the well-known phrase, "for better and for worse, in sickness and in health," yet how many couples consider the true depths of those phrases? If we're honest, most of us assume there will be little "for worse" and "in sickness," partially because we hope our spouse will do whatever is necessary in order to remove the worst parts of *themselves* in order to make the marriage (i.e., *us*) happy. When that doesn't happen, a naive spouse may throw the vows back at a partner who isn't meeting his or her needs: "You promised to accept me as I am! Why should I change? If you really loved me, you'd give in to my discomfort and anxieties. You'd put up with my limitations. You'd change—for me." These are not loving statements from a mature adult, but rather a manipulative way for a child in an adult's body to get their needs met on their own terms.

Such spouses believe one of the greatest fallacies about marriage: that it exists for our happiness. **Marriage isn't about making us happy, stable, or complete. Marriage is about growing us into better people.** Happiness, stability, and completion are welcome byproducts of a healthy marriage, but they're not the ultimate purpose of marriage—so don't make them so!

4. Don't fear the crucible.
Gridlock is a fearful place to live, and it's made even more menacing by the fact that resolution seems to recede into a distant horizon. When people believe that the only possible outcome to a troubling situation is for their spouse to come around to their own way of thinking, that marriage will be stuck in place until one spouse decides to leave. But this gridlock can be harnessed to help grow you. The mechanism for that growth is hidden in the constant push and pull of our desire for separateness (be our own person) versus our need for togetherness (experience companionship).

In Dr. Schnarch's excellent book *Passionate Marriage*, he refers to gridlocked conflict as a "crucible" of marriage.

These crucibles are "severe tests of our selfhood and personal integrity that are built into emotionally committed relationships." Whether you want it to or not, marriage fully reveals you to your spouse and to yourself. The crucible of marriage ensures that will happen.

So if conflict and the crucible aren't curable, what's your recourse? Essentially, you and your spouse will respond in one of these ways:

- Domination or Submission
- Withdrawal (physically or emotionally)
- Growth

This is the crucible. When you're considering how to respond to conflict that's put a complete stop on your marriage, you're in the crucible—a white-hot moment where your reaction will determine much about your future.

When one spouse enters into such a crucible, the other spouse only has a few options: go into their own crucible, manipulate the spouse so they'll return to their former ways of being, or allow the relationship to fail. This happens as a simple cause and effect. When a wife enters a crucible and must come to terms with herself and her marriage, she disrupts the status-quo. The system of marriage loses equilibrium, and the husband is necessarily forced to respond in order to bring balance back to the relationship.

To frame this another way, when you and your spouse experience gridlock and perpetual issues, you are presented with the choices of:

- Giving up on yourself.
- Giving up on your spouse and your marriage.
- Growing and developing a better and more real you.

In reading this book, you hopefully now know the right answer.

5. Make a choice.
In gridlock, each spouse faces a two-choice dilemma: do something fearful (e.g., rock the boat, speak up, initiate sex, etc.) or endure the problems that arise from inaction. Unhappiness within marriage tends to stem from the latter choice—and choosing not to choose is still a choice. By opting for denial, you've ultimately chosen misery and anxiety. But if you opt for action, you're choosing growth.

Unfortunately, resolving gridlock is never that simple. The foundational problem with gridlock is that both spouses have to make a choice in order to resolve the conflict, but each spouse wants to make both choices themselves. In other words, they want what they want and they want their spouse to also want what they want. When both spouses act this way, that's a marriage going nowhere fast.

Far too many couples I counsel suffer from "choosing" choice #1: give up on yourself. This can take the form of avoidance through compromise or relational laziness. It's a choice for those who don't choose anything. In hopes that the issue will resolve itself given enough time, they make no choice and effectively choose to cave in or give up. And how confidence-building and maturing is it to cave in or give up out of exhaustion?

"But Dr. Allan, haven't we been told that marriage is about compromise?"

Cultural wisdom isn't always correct. I define compromise as "that moment when each party goes away equally unhappy." Couples don't really compromise, do they? One caves in to the other. Consider your own marriage as a case study. In order to resolve a major moment of conflict, how often has your spouse caved in to you, or vice-versa? Many of us give in to others as a way to manage our anxiety in relationships and to quickly resolve conflict. But it doesn't really resolve, does it? Caving in allows room for bitterness to thrive. Caving in is a Band-Aid over a deep wound. Caving in damages the relationship.

Caving in leads to a scorekeeper marriage. When one spouse gives in to the other's desires, the compromising spouse makes a mental note of what was given so that they can later request something of like value in return. The "compromising" spouse expects reciprocal compromising—which isn't really what compromising is about. Such compromise gives now in order to demand later.

For instance, a husband may think, "We went to her parents last weekend. The least she could do for me is make time for sex tonight." A wife may think, "He played golf all day on Saturday. The least he could do for me is help clean up the house today." Some couples may speak these expectations, but more often than not they quietly reside within and bury the marriage in grave, hidden anxieties. In such exchange-based relationships where "keeping score" is a priority, nothing about the relationship will ever be fair. Plus, the energy wasted by constantly tallying "what's due me" can be much better applied elsewhere.

True compromise can only occur when two equally powerful and mature people can both clearly state their needs without an attachment to outcome. Then a solution can be jointly discovered that's satisfactory to both partners. Grown-ups don't need to cave in to one another because they know better ways to resolve conflict and manage their own anxieties at the same time. Mature adults can put the needs and wants of those they care about above their own desires, but can do so from a differentiated and unattached place, and not because they need that person's approval or because they need to feel better about themselves.

A true sign of growth is knowing that what you want for your spouse is what they want for themselves. Once you've finally achieved that kind of maturity, the gridlock you've been facing shifts just enough so that you can start to see your way to a better marriage soon.

6. Hold on to yourself.

Gridlock happens, and it will happen again. There's no way around it, but there is a way through it. The hard part is that going through gridlock means *growing* through gridlock, yet most of us tend to desire the end result of maturity without enduring the struggle to become mature. We want the rewards without the work. But there's no simple, easy way toward maturity. It has to be earned, and one of the prime ways you can learn maturity is to hold on to yourself.

Holding on to yourself means learning about yourself, confronting yourself, and shifting to self-validation by taking better care of yourself through self-soothing. It's a process of self-mastery and self-control that results in a more mature you and a more mature marriage.

After all, if you're unable to take care of yourself first, how can you expect to take adequate care of your spouse, children, and other people who are important to you? Put another way, how can you give from what you don't have?

If you feel worthless, pathetic, lazy, ugly, exhausted, or any other number of negative attitudes, your relationships will ultimately resemble what you feel within. On the other hand, if you take the right steps to care for yourself (which *isn't* being selfish), you will have more to give to others because you lack nothing and need nothing in return. Through setting proper boundaries, growing yourself up, learning to relax, and enjoying life as it happens, you will love yourself better, so you can love others better too.

Communicating better doesn't necessarily mean communicating more. Rather, it means being honest and vulnerable with what you share with your spouse. The myth of better communication equaling a better marriage sits under the umbrella of a much greater myth that dominates our culture, one that so many people take as truth that it's almost blasphemous to say otherwise—and especially for a licensed therapist to put into print.

12 Myth:
I must work on my marriage

Truth:
The marriage works on you

"Honey, would you mind coming to the bedroom? There's something I'd like you to see."

Ted rose from the recliner he always sat in after getting home from work. His wife Megan had been fairly quiet for a while. He was curious what she'd been up to. *Maybe it's something fun that involves neither of us wearing clothes.* Ted's mind wandered toward the possibilities, but then he opened their bedroom door.

"What *are* you doing?" he asked.

Megan just smiled, her eyes peeking from above a full-length mirror she held in front of her.

"Are you naked behind there?"

She didn't reply.

"What's this all about? This is, well, weird."

"Just look at yourself, Ted. Do you see what I see?"

"I don't know what you're talking about, Megan. I see a middle-aged dude who's quickly getting annoyed with this game. Unless you really are naked behind that, I'm going back to the living room."

"Just wait, Ted. Wait. Really look at yourself. Do you see anything wrong with yourself?"

Ted paused and tried to understand what his wife was asking him, but the longer he stood there in silence, the higher his heart rate became. "Megan, this is stupid. Please put that mirror down."

Megan didn't budge.

"If you don't put that thing down, I'm going to take it from you."

Megan still didn't move, so Ted grabbed the mirror out of her hands then held it up in front of himself, mirror-side facing out. "Why don't you answer the question now? What do you see in the mirror? Do *you* see anything wrong with yourself?"

Megan, fully clothed, remained quiet.

Much more angrily than he intended, Ted replied, "How about I tell you what I see is wrong? And then I'll share what I think you need to do to fix it. I guess you were right. We did need this mirror—and this ridiculous little exercise. Because you know what I see in the mirror? It's obvious: we need to work on our marriage."

Stop working on your marriage

I don't believe that any married couple who walks through my office doors needs to work on their marriage.

Shocking, right? Shouldn't a trained marriage counselor want his clients to work on their relationships? Isn't that the sole reason for their visit and my existence?

Well, yes, but I still don't want my clients to work on their relationships—at least not at the beginning. I don't want my clients to work on their relationships until they understand one foundational truth about marriage:

You don't work on the relationship; the relationship works on you.

Working on your marriage—this is a major marriage myth that's been passed down to us from commonly accepted practice: if the marriage is suffering, you need to work on it.

Of course, I agree that you certainly shouldn't let a failing marriage fail, but working on the marriage (which all too often subtly means "my spouse needs to change") tends to amplify problems instead of offering real solutions. Allowing the marriage to work on you is the better—yet much more challenging—perspective to take.

More than just verbal gymnastics, allowing your marriage to work on you shifts the balance of responsibility from your spouse to yourself. Choosing to mature yourself will likewise grow your marriage. Instead of constantly pointing a finger at how your spouse may have wronged you, you will begin to see your own culpability for a struggling marriage.

What I'm trying to say in so many words is that, as a matter of fact, the major problem of your marriage is…well…*you*. I'm sorry to be the bearer of bad news, but I tell you this from a place of care and concern.

For what it's worth, I'd tell your spouse the same thing.

The mirror of marriage
For all of its amazing benefits, marriage has an insidious way of bringing you face-to-face with your own shortcomings and failures. Because spouses share their lives with each other, they know exactly which buttons to push in order to cause particular reactions. They also know where the nuclear option is located, and they'll threaten its usage if necessary.

Note: *Threatening the nuclear option does not make for a healthy marriage.*

But don't we sometimes feel pressured into these defensive maneuvers? Among the most repeated phrases I hear in my office are, "He made me," or, "She made me." These spouses often feel as if their actions were the sole responsibility of their spouse's actions. But these reactions reveal far more about the people having them than it does their spouses.

Why? Perhaps we don't like being confronted with who we really are. If there's one thing that marriage is incredibly good at, it's revealing our true selves, whether we want such exposure or not.

Marriage is a mirror held up by our spouse, but instead of trying to work on who we see reflected, we yell at our spouse to put the mirror down, then we blame them for buying the mirror in the first place. Or we pick up the mirror, hold it up to our spouse, and point out their every flaw. All of this amounts to grand posturing and a stubborn refusal to let marriage work on you.

Think of it this way: if everyone's holding up a mirror to hide their true selves, the marriage is a mirage.

In choosing to no longer blame your spouse for your relationship problems, you will allow yourself and your marriage to mature. By taking personal responsibility for your own words, actions, and (perhaps most importantly) your reactions, you will begin to witness the transformation of your marriage—without the need to ever go nuclear.

Take the mirror you face toward your spouse and turn it around. This is where the real work of allowing the marriage to work on you begins.

Expose Yourself Before Marriage Exposes You

The best way to fight with your spouse is naked.

Now, before you start stripping down the next time your spouse's voice begins to rise (although that would be one way to end the conversation), I'm not talking about actual nakedness. Learning to control your seemingly uncontrollable lizard brain requires exposing yourself. When you went into your marriage, you likely had one of two basic attitudes regarding what your marriage would do *for you*: entitlement or exposure.

Entitlement is the *Jerry Maguire* "You complete me" expectation of marriage. An attitude of entitlement essentially says, "You make life better for me. You make me feel secure. You make me feel good about myself. You will take care of my needs. You are the best thing for me because of what you provide to me."

Such entitlement expects reciprocity. "When I give to you, you owe me. When I share with you, you have to share with me. If you don't share with me, I won't share with you. If I get personal first, you have to make me feel secure so I can trust you." Few people would ever voice these expectations, but if we could read between the lines of their marital conversations and actions, these are the expectations we would deduce.

Because entitlement focuses so heavily on the other person, an entitled spouse approaches his or her relationship problems from that others-focused perspective. Spouses with an attitude of entitlement will think, "What is wrong with my spouse? What do they need to change about themselves (or what can I try to change in them) so I can experience relief and comfort?"

Again, it's important to remember that you shouldn't be considering whether or not your spouse fits this description.

The real question you should ask yourself is whether or not *you* fit this description. Have your thoughts, words, and actions revealed an attitude of entitlement?

From my vantage point as a licensed therapist, we all suffer from this malady. Though its degree of severity differs from person to person, we all enter marriage with a certain amount of entitlement. In fact, a major way marriage matures us is by eroding entitlement, like a rough stone made smooth by thousands of waves over years, decades. Replacing an attitude of entitlement is not an overnight process. It takes time and intentional thought and action.

So how can you live from a place of less entitlement in your marriage?

Fight entitlement with exposure

An attitude of exposure is the direct opposite of an attitude of entitlement. An exposed spouse says, "I choose you because you will reveal me. Our relationship will expose my personality quirks, my character defects, and the immature ways I relate to you and others. I understand that you don't do this on purpose or to hurt me. Rather, it's the natural result of a committed marriage. Because of our relationship, I have the opportunity to see myself in a new way. I'm provided the chance to confront the person I've spent most of my life trying to escape: me. But if I'm willing to address what our marriage exposes about me, I can mature myself and see our marriage enjoy more love and passion than ever before."

Which of these two attitudes seems more natural?

By far, many of us go into marriage with an attitude of entitlement. We could blame our culture, our friends, our parents, or even our religion, but there's little changing where this notion of relational entitlement began. It leads to millions of couples getting happily married every year only to discover a few years down the line that their spouse is *not* going to meet their deepest needs, and in fact never will.

Choosing to expose yourself is not a natural response in marriage (or to anything, really). But choosing to live from an attitude of exposure is the best way to grow yourself up in your marriage. Instead of seeing marriage as a place where you are completed, a person who is growing sees marriage as the most important place that their incompletion is exposed. Aside from your relationship with your children, no other relationship will expose your incompleteness more than your marriage.

That's why you bristle so often and so forcibly when your relationship with your spouse—the one who's supposed to always be in your corner—reveals your weaknesses, needs, and relational and emotional immaturity. We don't speak it aloud, but our thoughts and actions in those revealing moments seem to instantly respond to our spouses with, "How could you do this to me?" That's the lizard brain (your emotional memories) reacting to the conflict at hand and choosing to fight, fly, or freeze. But if you can realize that your first reaction is more often emotionally based than logically based, you can begin to live from a place of exposure. Instead of trying to discover how your spouse needs to change to meet your needs, you can begin asking the much more challenging questions: "What does this situation expose about me?" and, "In what ways do I need to change and grow to more effectively love my spouse and myself?"

Choosing to be emotionally naked within your marriage may be the most challenging yet most rewarding decision you can make for both yourself and your spouse. Such nakedness means those three words most men fear and most women work in vain to elicit from their husbands: "Share your feelings." Emotional nakedness equals honesty, openness, and vulnerability in all things with your spouse. It's also not a state of being that most marriages quickly achieve. Rather, a spouse must choose to be emotionally naked again and again until such vulnerability becomes an ingrained habit.

Are You Hiding?
Revealing who you truly are can be a daunting task, especially if you've grown accustomed to wearing different masks for different people. While some of this is natural—you don't act the same way around your boss as you do your close friends—most of it is a result of fear.

One illustration about revealing one's true self occurs at the end of *The Wizard of Oz*. Dorothy reaches her final destination and meets the All-Powerful Wizard, but Toto reveals the real man behind the grand illusion. Still choosing to believe his own hype, the Wizard memorably says, "Pay no attention to that man behind the curtain." In your marriage, all of your work to prevent your spouse from ever truly knowing who you are amounts to consistently telling them, "Pay no attention to that person behind the curtain." You hide your true self because you you fear what will happen when people know the real you. You want people—and especially your spouse—to believe the hype.

And even when your spouse momentarily glimpses your true self, you have a tendency to react just like the Wizard. After all, you've lived so long with your illusion of yourself that you've begun to believe it as truth, but you fail to realize that your illusion of self is what's contributing to your relationship problems!

Another way to approach this issue is to ask yourself, "How can I stop letting my internal marketing department run my life?" You intuitively know that every ad campaign that touts "new, more, better" is really only trying to sell you something. Whatever you purchase as a result of that ad will not meet your every need, but contemporary ads sure make it seem like their products will do just that.

We tend to live our lives as if they were ads for our souls. If you don't believe me, consider the "ad" you ran 24/7 when you dated your spouse. Once you married, did they get what your promo advertised? Did you receive what they advertised? This is a cynical way to understand intimate relationships, but there's a thread of truth in it. Instead of revealing our authentic selves in dating relationships, we tend to let our internal marketing departments run wild. For many, this department keeps pretty busy even during the marriage.

But marriage has a way of revealing who we really are. Marriage is Toto, pulling back the curtain to show what we fear the world will one day discover about us. Yet it's this flawed and utterly human person—the Authentic You—who has the most opportunity to truly connect with your spouse.

When the marriage truly begins working on you, you'll notice its effects in many facets of your relationship, but those changes will likely be nowhere more apparent than in the bedroom.

13: Myth:
Sex is important but not essential

Truth:
Sex is essential to marriage

As a book with *Naked* in the title, this chapter was inevitable. Now it's time to finally shed your literal fig leaves.

I purposefully placed this chapter towards the end of the book because a mutually fulfilling sexual relationship within your marriage centers on everything we've discussed up to this point. You must know yourself and better understand your relationship with your spouse before true sexual intimacy can even occur.

First, let's assess your sex life. If I had to guess, you're probably in one of the three categories suggested by Dr. David Schnarch:

- The sexually barren
- The sexually average
- The blessed few

Membership within these categories has less to do with anatomy and drive than it does with each spouse's mental, emotional, physical, and spiritual health. It *is* possible that your marriage can rise to be included in the blessed few, but that requires the kind of hard self-work that's been discussed throughout this book. Because sex is not just a fun act and is actually a much deeper revelation of who you are, discovering and discarding the metaphorical fig leaves you've hidden behind for so long will make you more sexually attractive and more sexually driven toward your spouse.

Unfortunately, our culture's general relationship *to* sex is anything but steady or realistic. Some believe that sex is the bedrock of every great marriage. If fantastic sex—or at least consistent sex—isn't a part of the relationship, the spouse must not be who you're really supposed to be with. Or, at the other end of the spectrum, some view sex negatively, as if it's dirty, sinful, gross, or weird. This kind of poor perception often derives from religious beliefs.

But both of these views skew too far to one side. Sex is neither the end-all, be-all of existence, nor is it to be feared as some "icky" mandate required within committed relationships. Within marriage, sex is a good gift given to us by God for our pleasure. And regardless of your view on sex in general, there's one issue that can't be denied: a healthy sex life is essential to a healthy marriage.

For sexually barren spouses, this chapter will shift your perspective from only considering sex in light of frequency. Though frequency is a sign of a sexually healthy marriage, frequency is not the goal. The goal is much larger than that—and once the larger goals are met, frequency will increase.

Furthermore, marriages with little to no sexual activity may suffer from emotional problems that manifest themselves physically in the bedroom. When either spouse carries resentment, bitterness, or disappointment into the bedroom, issues like erectile dysfunction, arousal difficulties, and the inability to experience orgasm may quickly follow. In other words, a physical problem may be more mentally or emotionally driven than anything else. After all, if it *is* just a physical problem, certain drugs and medical procedures exist to help with these particular issues. Viva Viagra, right?

For sexually average couples, their plight doesn't appear as dire as the sexually barren, but their marriages can benefit greatly by having a healthier sexual relationship with each other. While they may experience times of deep connection through sex, they may also feel stuck in a rut or as if they're always trying to recapture the glory of former days.

For the blessed few, problems may still exist. Both spouses may have high sex drives, or one or both spouses may be using sex as a way to appease themselves or "resolve" conflict. Even when frequency is high, such a sexual relationship could be masking other issues.

In other words, all of us likely have issues when it comes to our sex lives, or we will at some time in the future. However, it *is* possible to reach the promised land of a healthy, frequent, consistent, and meaningful sex life with your spouse. But you have to stop considering sex by itself, as if it's just something that happens independently of every other aspect of your life. To become one of the blessed few who enjoy sex for the right reasons, you must be more present, not only during sex, but in the entirety of your life.

Now, let's consider the deeper meaning of sex within marriage. I believe sex is a symbol for how you live your life, and that means a better life will lead to better sex.

Sex as A Symbol

It should come as little surprise that sex can be a symbol for life. After all, where else but in the bedroom, naked as the day you were born, is there *more* potential for anxiety and rejection? Hundreds of fears can pass through our minds when the possibility of sex is near:

- Is she in the mood tonight?
- Why won't he just hold me for at least a few minutes before we start?
- Why doesn't she ever initiate sex?
- Am I sexy to him?
- Does she even like what I'm doing?
- Does he even know what he's doing?

I'm sure you (and your spouse) could add a few more bullet points. We *all* have our issues, but what's so troubling is that most of us tend to leave those issues in our minds, never to be resolved, because we fear the consequences for speaking those fears to the one person who could help quell them—or at least help us discover a mutually agreeable solution.

Even when we do get past our fears and admit our anxieties to our spouses, another problem presents itself: expected reciprocity. In other words, when we share, we expect our spouse to likewise share. If it's deep, personal, and revealing, we expect to hear something just as deep, personal, and revealing about them. It's a kind of subtle manipulation that effectively says, "I've given of myself; now you owe me something of like value in return." We tend to see intimacy as a tit-for-tat exchange of goods. We reveal ourselves in the hopes of receiving acceptance and validation from our spouses, as well as similar, personal disclosures from them.

After all, isn't revealing the truth about ourselves the basis for intimacy? Yes, but revealing that truth should not cost your spouse anything. Remember, part of growing yourself up in your marriage means not having an attachment to the outcome when you stand up for yourself.

Can you see how this plays itself out in sex? Our approach to sexual intimacy often depends on reciprocity.

To be blunt, our sex lives reveal our unspoken expectations: "I'll do you, then you do me." But what if what's being "done" to you isn't what you want? Does that mean it's time to bail on the marriage?

Being intimate doesn't mean that you always get the response you want. A healthy marriage is an interdependent relationship where neither spouse always gets what he or she wants, but where both spouses get what they need. A resilient marriage forms when both spouses can learn how to function independently so that their time together can be electrifying. As I've said before, learning to live apart together is integral to a thriving marriage. It's even more important to a thriving sex life.

When you can learn how to successfully confront yourself, challenge yourself to do what's right, and earn your own self-respect, you will develop a right attitude toward sex. You will learn how emotional nakedness leads to more confident *actual* nakedness that's magnetically attractive to your spouse.

The Sex Laboratory
Sex provides an amazing laboratory for practicing and strengthening nearly every principle we've covered so far. In fact, at its core, the answer to having a better sex life within your marriage is the same answer I've been suggesting all along: you must take responsibility for growing yourself up. You must learn how you can be more you. You must discover your Authentic Self and shed the fig leaves of lies, fears, anxieties, and doubts.

This may be difficult to read for some, but it's necessary: you may be dousing the flames of sexual passion and desire in your marriage by the way you're living your life. Remember, sex is not an event that's separated from everything else in your life. Sex is intimately connected to who you are and how you live your life.

I know what you may be thinking now: "So how is marriage a sex laboratory?"

Consider this:

- Sex is a great place to practice being a hundred percent present and taking the lead for your own life.
- Sex can help you become conscious of shame, insecurities, and self-limiting beliefs, but it can also help you eradicate them.
- Since the majority of us are pretty wounded sexually, being more present during sex is a great way to utilize the personal growth process of marriage.
- Sex is an ideal space to explore passion and risk-taking.
- Sex gives you the opportunity to embrace your masculine or feminine self and explore sexual polarity with your spouse.
- Being more present in sex can help you get to rejection quickly.
- Sex is a powerful way to practice being self-reliant, self-soothing, and just plain healthy.
- Sex and our sexuality cannot be separated from our daily lives, nor can our daily lives be separated from sex.

These principles can be used to create a great life for yourself and your spouse, as well as help you both experience mind-exploding sex like you've only dreamed of. To that end, let's discuss what turns on women and men. Knowing this will help both spouses learn what they may need to change about themselves and their own perspectives on sex so that a better sex life can soon be aroused.

What turns on a woman?
Had this been a chapter unto itself, I can imagine every man turning to it first.

Often, men think they know what turns their wives on. Just as often, they're wrong—or at least what worked *then* isn't working now, and men are left confused, frustrated, and going to bed unsatisfied. The biggest mistake men tend to make is to assume women are turned on by the same things they are, like physical attractiveness or touch. Or men believe that women are turned on by stereotypes of what turns on women: money, gifts, or just about any "attractive" quality that makes a woman fall for a man in a romantic comedy. Few men have the nerve to admit that they have *no idea* what turns their wives on, so they try as many different things as possible in order to discover what works—at least for today.

In my opinion, what essentially turns on a woman is much more basic: trust equals lust.

In other words, this idea from Dr. Robert Glover says that for a majority of women, they're turned on by a partner whom they can trust. How a woman feels when she is with a man is the primary determining factor in whether or not she experiences attraction and sexual desire. Her attraction is not ultimately about a man's looks, income, or job title. It's about *relationship*, which is why a husband being present in the home and in her life is a huge determining factor of a wife being turned on. A wide variety of complex factors also affect attraction (like early life experiences), but long-term connection and attraction is highly influenced by a woman's trust level.

For instance, if a man's wife has seemed to lose interest in sex with him over time, it's likely that he's either never given her a reason to trust him or he's killed whatever trust she once had in him. This doesn't mean that her trust can't be re-earned, but it will likely be a challenging (i.e., growing) process for that man.

What turns on a man?
It's little surprise to anyone that men are visually wired. One glimpse of a typically covered-up part of her body, and a vast majority of men are ready to jump into bed and get things moving. However, most men are also turned on by something else that's just as attractive, but that doesn't stem from external appearance.

A confident woman who knows who she is, isn't afraid of her femininity, and desires to spend time with her husband is often quite appealing to her husband. A woman who carries herself with respect and exudes beauty (which is unveiled, not put on) will capture and enrapture the thoughts of most men. Self-respect in a woman is sexy, which is why everything we've discussed about learning who you are and choosing to stand up for yourself is so important to a healthy sex life.

But there's one more thing that almost without fail will always turn on a man: a sexually turned-on woman. When a woman is able to let go and allow herself to be fully turned on sexually, a man can't help but to be likewise turned on by her.

Can you see how this kind of reciprocity is healthy? How the two genders can feed off one another's passion in a caring and fun way? Instead of trying to cater to one another or please each other, a turned-on husband and a turned-on wife can, rather naturally, have their sexual needs met.

When inner nakedness matches outward nakedness, the real fun begins.

For the women, consider reading Appendix E: Six To-Dos for Great Sex.

For the men, consider reading Appendix F, Three Rules for Great Sex.

14 Truth:
You can have a naked marriage

Marriage is designed to show you, you. Healthy marriages don't survive and thrive because each person works on the marriage, as if it were some third-party entity separate from each spouse. Rather, healthy, naked marriages flourish because each spouse works on him or herself and allows the marriage to work on them.

No other relationship in your life lays you as emotionally bare and starkly naked as a true marriage of honest equals does. But such a marriage requires an immense amount of intentionality, vulnerability, trust, faith, conversation, tears, conflict, conflict resolution, and the dogged ability of each spouse to remove their fig leaves of shame over and over and over again.

In other words, it's hard work to get naked.

After reading through the major myths about marriage I've covered, you might be overwhelmed. It's my hope that at least some of what you've read resonated with you. But with so much information and advice, I know it's challenging to attempt trying something new in your marriage when so many options abound.

So try this: go back to the one or two chapters that caused you to pause and consider your place within your marriage. What spoke to you on a deep level about how you could grow yourself so you could witness relational growth in your marriage? Skim or re-read those chapters, then begin to implement a few of my suggestions. Test what I've said. See what works for you. Surprise your spouse with different behaviors. Surprise yourself with different motivations.

Don't let this book become yet another book you place on a shelf to never read again. I ardently believe in its precepts and practicality, and hundreds of my clients have seen the benefits. Once you've witnessed growth in one particular area of your life and marriage, open the book to another chapter that spoke to you and repeat the test.

Don't make working on yourself in order to strengthen your marriage harder than it needs to be. Take one or two steps at a time, see if they help, then take one or two steps more. In time, I hope you'll be able to look back upon your trail of personal and relational growth and see the discarded remains of dozens of fig leaves.

Now, are you ready to get naked?

Appendix A:
Three Surprising Ways to Live a Better Story

Great lives are not built on great marriages. Rather the reverse is true. Great marriages are built on the foundation of two great lives, where each spouse chooses to write a compelling story with how they live their lives. Those compelling stories are attractive and often add the missing ingredient to a marriage gone stale.

But far too many of us have fallen for the fallacy that once we're married, we *must* live as if our spouse is our only priority, or as if our marriage (or our kids) define us. While your spouse and children should be vitally important to your life, they're still but a smaller aspect of your overall existence. What makes you, you is more than your family, more than your responsibilities, and more than your job.

If you've found yourself stuck in a rut of monotony within your marriage, I encourage you to focus on three particular—and surprising—ways to live a better life story as suggested by Dr. Robert Glover: pursue your passions, form same-sex friendships, and engage in regular exercise.

1. Pursue your passions.
Living passionately means working and playing at what makes you completely happy and fulfilled. Take a moment and honestly ask yourself, "When was the last time I pursued what makes me happy?" For many people in passionless marriages, one spouse (or both) has never

discovered his or her true passions in life. They may tell themselves that their husband, wife, or kids is their passion but then experience a disconnect when they realize they're still left unfulfilled in some unnamable way. For others, they know what their passions are, but they've sacrificed pursuing those passions because the marriage or parenting has taken precedence. Essentially, they'e given up on taking care of themselves in order to take care of others—which can quickly lead to fused relationships.

Fused systems fear passion. Passion threatens fused systems because passion is volatile and unpredictable. Passion can shoot a person off in any number of directions, potentially leaving other members of the system behind. Passion can inspire a person to lead a revolution, join a monastery, cycle across a continent, sacrifice everything for a business idea, or fall madly in love. Because of this unpredictability, fused systems are extremely resistant to personal passion—which should be all the more reason for spouses in fused relationships to begin pursuing their own passions. Something *will* change when you begin to honestly pursue your passions.

Only grownups can be passionate. Growing up requires you to regularly ask yourself, "What do I want?" and "What feels right to me?" If you never ask yourself these questions, you will never find passion. Most people I work with have no idea what they want or need. They've spent so much time and energy taking care of everyone else that they have little to no idea who they are or how to find out. And it can be doubly frustrating because they believe they should be fulfilled, yet they aren't, and they can't quite put their finger on why that is. Again, I believe it's because they've fallen for the lie that all of our needs should be met within marriage and/or parenting—as if validation can only come from external sources.

But I also believe that design equals purpose and purpose equals passion. Each of us is unique and beautifully designed with specific strengths and capabilities. To find your passion, discover your design. What do you excel at? What are you consistently compelled to do, seek, or think about? As you work toward discovering your design, your purpose will emerge. And when you live with purpose, therein lies your passion.

One last note about pursuing your passions: don't focus on finding your one passion. You will likely have several at one time, or several over the course of your life. Whatever you do, don't stop searching for your passions.

If you've struggled with pursuing what you're passionate about it, consider implementing these two simple action steps right now:

- Stop doing anything you aren't doing passionately.
- Start doing everything you do with passion. Shave with passion. Do the dishes with passion. Work with passion. File your taxes with passion. Take a walk with passion. Listen to music with passion. Have sex with passion.

If you're feeling stuck and passionless, consider going on a "vision quest." Go into the wilderness and spend time alone. While there, ask yourself, "What would I most like to be doing if I could be doing anything right now?"

Dream your dream, then live it.

Like a moth to a flame, your passion will attract a healthy spouse. Your spouse may want to be turned on by you, but without passion, there's nothing to light their fire.

2. Form same-sex friendships

Without the foundation of same-gender friends, a relationship with a spouse will become needy and codependent. A spouse can't meet all of your relationship needs, nor should they try. That's a recipe for either a lifeless or short-lived marriage. When you have healthy relationships with friends of the same sex, you don't put pressure on your spouse to meet needs they'll never be able to meet.

Again, I think culture (and specifically romantic comedies) have caused us to believe the lie that our spouses *must* be our best friends. The sentiment sounds great, but it's severely misguided. I don't believe a person of the opposite sex can truly be a best friend.

When couples meet with me for marriage counseling, I stress the importance of good same-sex friends. Men need masculine connections and women need feminine. No matter how good of a friend someone of the opposite sex may be, he or she can't connect with you or understand you in the way a friend of the same sex can.

This suggestion is often the most difficult for men. For guys, it's often easier to meet women and form relationships with them than it is to meet other men and form healthy, close friendships. To make matters more daunting, men must consistently work to form new friendships with other guys as their life stages change (marriage, children, divorce, work, moving, etc.), while also working to maintain the close friendships they've already formed. But the ultimate benefits to your marriage from forming healthy same-sex friendships can't be overrated. It's integral that you have a best friend or three of your same gender so that you're not looking to your spouse for answers, help, and encouragement that only another guy can provide.

As they're naturally more relational, women often have less trouble with this suggestion, but forming same-sex friendships is equally important to women for many of the same reasons.

3. Engage in regular and *strenuous* exercise.
You'll notice the emphasis on strenuous. I'm a great advocate for regular, strenuous exercise because of its many benefits, both to your physical and emotional well-being. At least three to five days a week, you should be regularly exerting yourself to the point of sweating. Your options are near limitless: run, bike, lift weights, play hoops, practice yoga, play tennis, do Pilates. Find what you enjoy and do it regularly and strenuously.

In some ways, our ancient ancestors were lucky because they got this kind of exercise on a daily basis just trying to survive. But cubicle farms and work-from-home employment has us sitting nearly dormant for far too long. Then after a long day of mostly sitting, what do most of us tend to do? Go home and sit some more, right in front of the TV, where hours fly by until it's time to *lie down* and go to bed—until we get up the next morning to go sit in our office—again. Now, that's a bit facetious, but it's also sadly true for far too many of us. Plus, the scary science behind our massive sitting problem keeps pointing to the fact that we all need to get up and exercise far more often and for longer than we think we should. And, as a busy professional with a family of my own, I know how difficult it can be to make time for regular exercise that gets your heart pumping. But, again, the benefits of scheduling consistent exercise are well worth whatever sacrifice you may have to make.

I'm not telling you anything you don't already know, but let's remember a few of the major benefits of regular, strenuous exercise:

- Helps prevent heart disease and diabetes, two challenging and deadly medical issues that afflict millions in the U.S.
- Keeps your shape in shape, which will make you feel better about yourself
- Decreases tiredness despite the fact that exercise itself may make you tired
- Aids with better sleep because your body needs to recuperate
- Enhances your mood as well-earned endorphins (the runner's high) flow
- Increases discipline in other areas of your life

Those are all very healthy benefits to choosing a lifestyle where regular exercise is a priority. However, one seemingly tangential benefit to exercising is one that I witness helping my clients time and time again: choosing a challenge over comfort.

Pursuing comfort over a challenge is the reason many turn to addictions like food, alcohol, and porn. It's also why they seek a spouse to fill them up. Additionally, trying to change a spouse (or waiting for that spouse to change) is the much more comfortable path than choosing to challenge and change yourself. That's why many married couples avoid conflict rather than lean into it. Such latent conflict may not be "comfortable," but it's considered more comfortable than the alternative, where the outcome can't be known and may not be what either party desires.

Those who seek comfort in life above all else are very likely never to find it. Furthermore, comfort-seekers have boring life stories, and boring life stories don't make for an attractive mate. Only through leaning into life's challenges will you grow, feel complete, and look deeply attractive to the opposite sex.

Start Writing a Better Story

> Pursue your passions.
> Form same-sex friendships.
> Engage in regular and strenuous exercise.

These are the three simple ways you can start writing a better story with your life. If you start feeling lethargic, unmotivated, depressed, addictive, or needy, see if you've been neglecting one or more of these suggestions. If so, consciously get them back into balance. Don't seek to check off these items like they were on a to-do list. Rather, seek to be consistent in your pursuit of these essential story elements.

When you're regularly applying these three key suggestions to your daily life, you will not only create a great story and be more attractive to your spouse, you will also make a difference to the planet. Living a great story allows you to give your gift to the world every day you're alive.

As you begin to feel "fuller" from a life that's better and more deeply connected both to yourself and to your personal relationships, you may find that you have more to give out of the overflow of your life. You can make decisions that cost you something without feeling like it's costing you much. You can make personal sacrifices to maintain healthy, mature relationships. With an "abundance" view of the world—where you realize that you already have everything you need—you can give fully of yourself without resenting others and without the need to control any outcomes.

Eventually, living a better story helps you find yourself, and once you know, appreciate, and love who you really are, your spouse *will* take notice.

Appendix B:
How to set smart boundaries

1. Don't allow others to treat you badly.
This is the cardinal rule of boundary setting.

If someone accidentally plants a foot directly on your toes, it's your job to say, "Excuse me! You're standing on my toes!" It is *not* your job to try to figure out *why* that person is standing on your toes before telling them to step off.

Yet this is how nice guys and those with pleaser mentalities often react to being treated badly. They may think to themselves, "What can I do to extricate myself from this situation without upsetting this person?" Or, they'll quietly seethe with resentment, wait until the other person moves, then casually say, "Oh, that's nothing" when the toe-stepper finally acknowledges their mistake.

Those who allow themselves to be consistently treated poorly by others tend to believe that everyone will treat them the way they treat everyone else. But that's a myth that needs to be discarded. It would be amazing to live in a world where people treated *everyone* the way they would like to be treated, but that's not the world in which we live.

People hurt people, sometimes on purpose, but most often without evil intent. When you allow yourself to be treated poorly—and especially by your spouse—you're essentially letting them off the hook for their bad behavior and allowing your inner bitterness to grow a strong, sturdy, and steady root.

Your prime responsibility in setting the right boundaries within your marriage (and your life) is to let people know what works for you and what doesn't. Don't assume they know or that they'll figure it out given enough time. They cannot read your mind, nor is it their responsibility to figure out what presses your buttons (or not).

Often, other people have little idea that they're crossing one of your boundaries. If provided insight into your boundaries, most people would gladly yield to your wishes and treat you the way you desire to be treated. But to get to that point, you must be vocal and preemptive when it comes to not letting others treat you badly.

When it comes to setting proper boundaries, don't stand for being stood on anymore.

2. Decide when, how, and when to set your boundaries.

As a child, your parents controlled your boundaries, from your crib to your first car. Those boundaries expanded over time (I hope) until you became an adult. Now, as an adult, one of the greatest yet most frustrating of privileges presents itself to you: absolute freedom. This includes the freedom to decide what kind of behavior you will accept from others, i.e., the freedom to set your boundaries on your schedule.

A common refrain from my clients while discussing boundary setting is, "How do I know where to set my boundaries?" This can be especially challenging for clients who have seldom (or never) thought about what it means to have healthy emotional boundaries within their relationships. Additionally, when a loved one tells a boundary-setting spouse that he or she *shouldn't* be setting a particular boundary, knowing where to set a boundary becomes even hazier.

When first learning how to set proper boundaries, the focus shouldn't be so much on *where* to set the boundary as *when* to set it. In other words, I believe it's more important to act soon rather than deliberate forever. Of course, you should give careful consideration to the specific types of boundaries you need in your life, but you should aim to implement those boundaries within a short timeframe. I believe quick action is helpful because setting boundaries is like creating a new product: you need iterations.

Every time you set a boundary, you learn from the process. Through the actual experience of setting a boundary and seeing how your loved ones react to that boundary (instead of just thinking about how they *might* respond), you learn where your personal boundaries actually exist and what feels right to you.

We're all different, so there's no one-size-fits-all recommendation I can give you to set the right boundaries in your life. All I can suggest is that you learn more about yourself and what you want out of life and your relationships—especially your marriage. Then set a few boundaries that seem appropriate, and even challenging, to you, and live with those boundaries for at least a month. In that time, you will learn better boundary setting through real-life experience. As you become more comfortable with this "new you," you will strengthen your boundaries, which may expand or contract depending upon what you've learned, who you are, and the particular life circumstances in which you find yourself. Just like relationships, boundaries are never meant to be rigid or stagnant. Your boundaries will shift throughout your life, but the important thing is to start setting proper boundaries as soon as you can.

3. Set boundaries from your Authentic Self.

Healthy boundary setting requires a healthy dose of "I" messages. To set boundaries from your core identity, ask yourself these two simple questions:

- What do I want?
- What feels right to me?

Unfortunately, married couples seldom ask themselves these questions, or they ask them from the wrong motivation. Some couples may think these questions are too selfish, as if by asking this, they're rejecting the idea that two become one. Other couples may ask themselves these questions on their way *out* of a marriage, as if the answer to a failing marriage is taking the common denominator to another marriage. These questions should not be considered in either light. Instead, spouses should honestly ask themselves these questions and answer them by carefully considering what they want *for themselves.*

Boundaries are about changing yourself, and you can't change yourself if you don't understand what's intrinsically important to you. When you finally discover answers to these questions, you must then learn how to hold on to yourself and how to act with integrity in light of your Authentic Self.

In other words, you have to learn how to withstand the pressure when other people in your life encroach upon your boundaries—some on purpose, but many haphazardly. Even more taxing, such pressure doesn't only occur from external sources. We can also be the chief invaders of our own boundaries through our own anxiety, guilt, and shame.

In my practice, I teach my clients that holding on to themselves means learning how to soothe their anxiety when presented with a troubling situation or even the worry that a problem may arise. This means coming to grips with all possible outcomes of a trying experience, from the good to the disastrous. Much of healthy self-soothing resides in self-motivation and self-talk. For instance, if a husband crashes his wife's car because of his lead foot, he could soothe the imagined, condemning voice in his head by choosing to focus on the past, positive aspects he's witnessed in his wife when he presented her with similar troubling information. She may very well get upset, but the man in this situation will better weather that small storm than exacerbate the problem by further arguing with his wife, denying culpability for the wreck, or choosing to ignore her altogether.

When you don't learn how to put self-soothing into practice, your own anxiety, guilt, and shame will negatively contribute to the situation at hand. Facing the music in this wreck of a situation isn't easy, but it's the grown-up thing to do, and if you've read this far, you know how important I think being grown up is to having a stellar marriage.

4. You are the sole definer of your boundaries.

Setting boundaries isn't about getting other people to act differently. Remember the healthy "me-first" mentality? Setting boundaries is about getting *yourself* to be different. When you significantly change, the way people treat you will likewise significantly change. Far too often, my clients get this process reversed. They try as hard as possible—whether overtly or passive-aggressively—to change their spouses for their own happiness. But as I've said time and again, you have to *change yourself* before you can expect change in your marriage.

Unfortunately, we don't live in a fair world. When my clients say things like, "She shouldn't treat me that way," or, "I would never do that to him," I have to remind them that the people in their lives will not treat them well simply because my clients think they should. It isn't the other person's responsibility to know how you want to be treated.

You are the only person responsible for how you want to be treated. You are the sole determinant of who can come inside your boundaries, when they're allowed to do so, what they're allowed to do while there, and how long they're allowed to stay. But setting your own boundaries isn't enough. You must vocalize them. You must train others how you want them to treat you.

Emotionally confident and healthy spouses show their partners how they expect to be treated within the marriage, then lovingly lead their spouses into that place with integrity. Boundary setting is not about controlling the other person or mandating your will above all else. It's also not about choosing your own boundaries and hoping that your spouse somehow gets the message over time. You must learn to speak up for yourself, which is often one of the most difficult aspects for a "boundless" person to begin doing when setting boundaries—especially within rocky marriages where the doing so can lead to so many unknowns.

5. You must be willing and able to remove yourself.
As a child, you couldn't choose to remove yourself from situations. You were forced to endure whatever may have been happening, then you likely tried to discover ways to prevent that same situation from reoccurring. Because of your lizard-brain memories, you likely still react to stress in the same way. Because of how ingrained these responses are, removing yourself may not even seem like an option to you.

Note: "removing yourself" doesn't necessarily mean separation or divorce. It could mean those things, but this covers a broad spectrum of responses, from the simple, "Call me back when you're in a better mood," to the final, "I'm leaving."

As an adult, you have full rights of refusal. You can refuse to comply with any situation that presents itself by removing yourself from that situation, whether temporarily or permanently. This is part of disallowing others to treat your poorly. Sometimes, the best answer to their poor treatment is a turned back. Other times, it may mean walking away.

Many of my clients don't consider this a viable option, mistakenly believing that to literally turn their backs on their spouses will only make their problems worse. But like I said before, when you can get to rejection quickly, that's when you can begin to see progress.

The refusal to remove yourself from trying situations makes you impotent. This "choice to not choose" renders you powerless, and because you intuitively know that you're ceding control to the other person in the relationship, you subconsciously attempt to gain it back through passive acceptance, subtle manipulation, threats, arguments, passive-aggressiveness, pouting, etc. Even though you effectively granted the power of the relationship to, let's say, your wife (by not being capable or willing to remove yourself from her), you're still trying to get her to act the way *you* want her to. It's not a balance of power; it's a seesaw that leaves you high and dry and seething on the inside.

Without a willingness or ability to remove yourself, you have no power to create change and to consequently affect the behavior of those around you. To set boundaries, you have to be willing to walk away—a little or a lot—when necessary. If you aren't willing to walk away from an intolerable or unsatisfactory situation, you have no power to change the situation.

Believe it or not, you can't be truly intimate with your spouse if you're not willing or able to remove yourself from her. If you don't know you can get out, you will put up walls, avoid, or keep trying to get her to change so you don't have to. Knowing that you can leave gives you the power to set clear boundaries and fully open yourself up to your spouse. But you can't simply give mental assent to this; you must actually be ready to physically remove yourself if the situation and your boundaries call for it.

6. Say "I" and keep it brief.
Boundaries beginning with "you" aren't boundaries; they're vain attempts at control.

"You never want to have sex anymore" is the wrong way to establish a boundary regarding your marriage's sex life. The fact of your statement may be true, but you cannot do anything to force your spouse to change his or her attitude about sex.

Instead, change yourself by changing the way you talk about your boundaries: "Sex is important to me, and I'd like us to find ways to have it more often." Your spouse may still take offense: "What is that supposed to mean?" but using "I" messages in this way is much less confrontational than accusing your spouse of no longer wanting to have sex.

Setting boundaries through "I" statements is important for all aspects of a marriage, and not just sex. A spouse shouldn't say, "You should stop yelling at me." Rather, he or she should say, "I don't like being yelled at. I will need to get off the phone with you if you keep yelling at me." That's the kind of boundary setting you should seek to accomplish: honest, to-the-point, focused on your own actions, standing up for yourself, and without attachment to the outcome of your decision.

To communicate how your spouse's actions or words are making you feel, say, "It is important to me that…." This is a powerful way to communicate your boundaries. Furthermore, starting a phrase with, "I want you to" and finishing the phrase with why you need that is a way to give people the option of cooperating with you:

- "I want you to talk more calmly with me, so we can resolve this issue."
- "I want you to tell me the truth in all situations, so I can trust you."
- "I want you to be more sexually available in our relationship."

An alternative method that serves the same purpose is to state your problem and ask your spouse to help be the solution: "I like living in a clean and clutter-free home. Can you help me keep it clean?" By focusing on your needs and not your spouse's shortcomings, you invite help rather than conflict. You don't accuse; you persuade.

Lastly, the most important part of using "I" messages is to keep it brief. When possible, use the two-sentence rule. State your boundary and how your spouse can respect that boundary, then let your spouse decide on his or her response. The more you talk and try to justify, argue, or defend your boundary, the less powerful you will begin to appear to them. Strong boundaries don't need verbal reinforcement.

7. Don't use a sledgehammer when a flyswatter will do.

Boundary setting is liberating, but sometimes it throws inner doors so wide open that my clients start setting boundaries like General Patton making war preparations. In other words, when a person's eyes are open to how boundaries can help in their marriage, they tend to come on too strongly when setting their first boundaries. Because of its newness and because they expect sizable pushback from their spouses in reaction to their own inner change, they feel the need to use a sledgehammer when a flyswatter will suffice. In my practice, I call this "Kamikaze Boundary Setting."

When setting boundaries, use only what resistance or strength is necessary to get the job done. Setting boundaries is an ongoing process where each boundary you set helps you understand what other boundaries you need to set and how to adapt your current boundaries. In other words, you will get better with practice. The same holds true for learning to use finesse when setting proper boundaries. You will learn when a sledgehammer is necessary (which ought to be rarely).

People respond best to boundaries set by a strong man or woman who can confidently and calmly say what he or she wants and what he or she won't accept. Effective boundary-setters show people how they expect to be treated (without manipulation, guilt, shaming, etc.) and then lovingly lead others there without attachment to outcome. Most people appreciate these kinds of powerful boundaries and will respectfully respond.

Choosing to respond with a larger weapon only escalates wars, and the greater the weapon, the greater the death toll. Don't wield your boundaries with an iron fist. More often than not, setting a boundary and confidently choosing to maintain it is powerful enough on its own.

8. Have no attachment to outcome.

Effective boundaries require zero attachment to outcome. From the outset of setting your boundaries, you *must* be willing to accept *whatever* happens as a result of those boundaries. When your boundaries can bear the brunt of any possible outcome, true change is possible in your relationship.

If one of your boundaries makes you walk away from your husband while he's treating you badly, he might throw a fit, call you names, storm off himself, say the relationship is over, or claim that you're being manipulative. (Note: when presented with a new boundary he can't manipulate, a persistent manipulator's greatest manipulation is to manipulate the other person through accusations of manipulation.)

You must be willing to accept whatever comes.

This is one of the reasons why getting to rejection quickly is an important aspect of marriage. Getting to rejection isn't placing the marriage on the brink of divorce, it's putting yourself fully out there to be either accepted or rejected. I know that this seems counterintuitive, but it's true. Setting proper boundaries is one of the most powerful ways to get to rejection quickly, but only if you're willing to face whatever the outcome is and stand up for your own boundaries.

In a strange way, in order to set powerful boundaries, you have to love your spouse enough to let them hate you sometimes.

9. Perform routine maintenance on your boundaries.

Our relationships would be so much easier if we could set such clear and strong boundaries just *once* and have them forever guard our hearts and minds against being used, abused, or neglected. Unfortunately, once you create a boundary, you have to maintain it. You can't assume that a person who knows your boundaries will never cross them again. People have short memories and strong habits.

Like an animal trapped in an electrified cage, given enough time and motivation, people will test your boundaries for possible weaknesses. They may not do it on purpose, but they will do it. Sometimes they'll do it to see if you'll follow through with what you said you would do, especially if boundary setting is new to you. Sometimes they'll test your boundaries because they don't like what it means for them. The sad but true part of boundary setting is that every time you set a boundary, you need to be prepared to set it again, with the same people, as often as necessary.

The best way to maintain your boundaries is the way you created your boundaries: speak up.

Speaking up is a loving but confident way to tell others precisely where you stand and where they stand in relation to you. Speaking up tells people exactly what you will and won't accept from them. Speaking up reveals what consequences they can expect from you if they continue to treat your poorly.

People in your life *must* know the consequences of treating you badly. For example,

- "When you talk to me that way, you're damaging our relationship."
- "If you verbally abuse me again, I'm going to go see a counselor."
- "If you continue your affair, I will divorce you."

It's that last consequence that can strike fear into any marriage, which is why threats of divorce or separation are too often thrown about long before such a drastic measure should even be considered. Yes, sometimes such a consequence *is* legitimate, but it shouldn't be used as an empty threat. In other words, don't choose the nuclear option unless you're ready to hit the big red button. If your spouse is having an affair, don't mention divorce unless you're ready to seek a divorce. Don't threaten separation unless you're ready to walk away from the relationship for a time. Your power to set effective boundaries resides in your willingness and ability to remove yourself.

When confronted with powerful consequences, a spouse may react by threatening, "Don't give me an ultimatum!" When people don't want to quit what they're doing, they don't respond well to ultimatums. After all, it requires them to make a choice when all they want is to keep the status quo—because the status quo is heavily in their favor. If they do make a choice, they know they'll have to reap the consequences of that choice, which isn't a favorable option to them. But all behaviors have consequences. If they choose to not choose, then they've made a choice, and you'll have a better idea whether divorce or separation is a viable option for you.

10. Move your boundaries.
Boundaries need both external and internal routine maintenance. As other people test the limits of your boundaries, so too will your inner life test your boundaries' limits. This means that from time to time you should reassess what you want out of life. This means growing up, listening to yourself, and being open to feedback from others. You may learn that you haven't clearly communicated your boundaries. Or you may have set such strict boundaries that you've effectively erected walls.

After checking in with yourself and those you trust, adjust your boundaries accordingly. Don't move a boundary just because one person doesn't like it, and don't move it to lessen possible repercussions. When you back off to manage your anxiety, that's not a mature adjustment—it's caving.

Remember that healthy boundaries are solid, but they're malleable. They can and should change over time. Your boundaries will be affected by those around you as well as by your Authentic Self. And as you'll recall, the more boundary-setting you do, the more effective you will be at creating and maintaining boundaries that serve the dual purpose of protecting you while still letting others in.

With smart boundaries, you can be an emotionally and spiritually healthy individual who thrives in your marriage and every other relationship in your life.

Appendix C:
Six steps toward fully revealing the Authentic You

The Authentic You isn't driven by a need to manage anxiety by controlling people and situations outside of yourself. When you live from the Authentic You, you can show up in life and in relationships with strength, courage, honesty, vulnerability, and transparency. You can let people get close to you, and you can handle feelings of separation. The Authentic You is passionate, lives up to your potential, and gives your gift to the world. The Authentic You can ascertain what is most needed in any given situation, has appropriate boundaries, and can clearly communicate needs.

Marriage is the perfect laboratory for you to discover and work on these traits.

1. Growing the Authentic You requires learning how to self-soothe.

Because most of what happens to you in life is outside of your control, just about anything can trigger anxiety:

- Long-forgotten childhood wounds are suddenly torn open in your current relationship.
- Guilt and shame wash over you because of past mistakes you can't release.
- A deep need to seek approval from others causes you to hide your true feelings.

- A desire to be perfect in the eyes of others results in untold stress that no one sees.

And those are just the larger internal issues we oftentimes overlook because we're so used to living with them on a daily basis. Mundane stressors like marriage, kids, friends, job, and extended family heighten opportunities for anxiety. And that's not even taking into consideration anxiety induced by current events, like terrorism, racism, and just about any other "ism" that happens to be in the news of the day.

Creating a list of what causes stress in your life may be an unending task, yet it's important that you define your main stressors. Consider these questions:

- What thoughts keep you up late?
- When your mind wanders, where does it naturally wander to?
- What topic(s) seem to arise most often in your conversations with your spouse? Your co-workers? Your friends? Your family?
- If you're a parent, what do you fear most for your child?
- Which people trigger stress when you know you have to talk or meet with them soon?

Identifying what brings anxiety into your life can help you better prepare to soothe yourself. The solution to anxiety is not to run away from it. The more you run, the more likely it is that that particular stressor will continue to increase in strength. Anxiety is real, but it won't kill you.

For practical ways to self-soothe, see Appendix D.

2. Growing the Authentic You requires honesty.

Strangely, with the couples I've counseled in the aftermath of an affair, the offended spouse is often more hurt by the fact that the wayward spouse *lied* to them rather than that they had sex with another person. There's something deeply intimate about truth, especially within a marriage.

Living from a place of genuine authenticity requires honesty *at all times*. But why is this so challenging for us to put into practice? Because we shade, omit, alter, distort, or change the truth to fit *our* needs, usually as an attempt to avoid conflict, disappointment, or judgment.

When you fail to tell the truth, the whole truth, and nothing but the truth in the courtroom of your marriage, you're lying under the oath you made at your wedding. Your sentence for such perjury is a distrustful relationship in which both spouses live as the person they think the other person wants them to be. It's a facade of a marriage predicated upon lies and half-truths. When you fail to be fully honest with your spouse, there's little opportunity for them to likewise be honest with you.

Being honest in your marriage means telling the whole truth. It means doing what you say you'll do. It means acting and speaking with integrity. The honest Authentic You is an open book who willingly chooses to share his or her thoughts and feelings—the good, the bad, and the ugly, no matter the outcome.

3. Growing the Authentic You requires letting go of your attachment to outcome.

Many of us are unaware of what we're truly attached to. When I work with a client who feels stuck, uncertain, or resentful about a relationship, I ask, "What would you do if you had absolutely no attachment to outcome in this situation?"

Silence hangs in the room for a second, and it seems to me as if they've never considered such a question before. After all, most of us always have a deeply personal attachment to the outcome of a particular situation. We often have such a vested interest in what may happen that it's difficult for us to fully remove ourselves. But such a client typically responds with a very simple and straightforward answer: "I'd tell her the truth."

Attachment distracts us from the simple, elegant solutions in life.

Notice that I didn't say easy. Often, making a choice in life without attachment to outcome is hard. It doesn't come naturally to us, but I promise that learning how to make choices without always seeking to control the situation is a prime way for you to discover and unleash your authentic self.

What are you attached to? Consider these questions, which can apply to lots of situations, not just your relationships:

- What do you often complain about?
- What agitates you?
- What makes you anxious?
- What do you try to control?
- What do you fear losing?
- What are you afraid of not getting enough of?
- Where do you keep getting stuck?
- What makes you feel confused?

When we have a deep attachment to the outcome of a particular situation or relationship, we're more likely to have increased anxiety. Releasing your attachment to outcome can greatly decrease your anxiety. Unfortunately, pain is an unavoidable part of life, and most suffering comes from our attachment to not wanting to experience pain.

Once we accept that life is sometimes painful and difficult, we can let go of our attachment to *not* feeling pain. When the inevitable pain of life strikes like a sudden hurricane, learning the art of self-soothing and growing up can help see you through to calmer seas.

4. Growing the Authentic You requires being a hundred percent present.

The Phone Stack game may be the best illustration of how we're seldom a hundred percent present in any of our relationships today. In The Phone Stack, people who dine out together all place their phones in the center of the table. The first one to reach for his or her phone must then pick up the check for the entire table. It's a smart and fascinating way to encourage face-to-face conversation in our heads-down, fingers-blazing, all-too-connected-but-still-so-lonely culture.

How often have you had dinner with your spouse, yet remember very little of what he or she said because all you could think about was the massive work project you had due in three days? How often has your mind wandered while speeding down the highway, only to get home and not really know how you got there? We are easily distracted, but we must strive to be more conscious.

To be conscious simply means to observe ourselves without judgment. Consciousness allows us to be aware of what we are thinking, feeling, and doing and therefore gives us the option to evaluate whether our responses are taking us where we want to go.

Consciousness allows you to:

- Be aware of how your actions affect others.
- Apply past experiences to current and future situations.
- Anticipate consequences and have empathy for other people.
- Listen (sometimes with amusement) to the chatter in your brain.
- Pay attention to your emotional impulses and decide how to act upon them.
- Follow your gut.
- Become aware of stress responses in your body.

For example, I am more reactionary, short-tempered, and impatient when I'm stressed or in a hurry. When I observe myself in these states, I simply ask myself, "What's going on?" Being aware of my current state and my reactions allows me to stay more conscious and to decide what I want to do about what I am observing. Perhaps I need to step outside and breathe deeply, walk around, or put off the conversation until I can be more present and engaged. The point is, when I'm aware I'm not a hundred percent present, I can take appropriate steps to become a hundred percent present—or at least closer to that mark than I was before.

When a situation triggers anxiety, realize that it presents important information about *you* and not about the triggering situation. Realize that you will keep bumping into this issue until you become conscious enough to pay attention to it. When you do, you will be free to move through life without having to face the same issues over and over again.

5. Growing the Authentic You requires maturing yourself.
Remember: growing up relationally and emotionally has little to do with your age.

When you were two or three years old, you began to separate yourself from your parents. What they termed rebellion was actually a good, proper, positive, and essential aspect of your development into a mature adult. This is when your differentiation began. At that young age, you started to distinguish yourself as a unique individual, separate from all others. That's why two-year-olds of every nationality often learn and lean on words like "no" and "mine." They're asserting their selfhood.

As the child matures, he or she becomes more aware of his or her own wants, needs, and purposes. This process should continue throughout adulthood, but many people seem to get stuck (or even go into reverse) when presented with their first serious romantic relationship.

Too often, people view other important people as an extension of themselves and view themselves as extensions of other people, especially in regard to family and spousal relationships. This lack of differentiation (growing up) is called "fusion" and results in all kinds of lizard-brain behaviors spurring selfish agendas and expectations:

- "You're my wife, so you should want to have sex with me whenever I want it."
- "You're my husband, so you should want to listen to me talk about my best friend's relationship problems."
- "You're my daughter, so you should call me each week to see how I am doing."

Undifferentiated, fused people often resort to control and manipulation as they project their expectations onto others. They feel resentful when others don't live up to their expectations, and they often react with aggression or passive-aggressiveness.

A grown-up is able to ask himself:

- "What do I want in this situation?"
- "What feels right?"
- "What is best for my spouse, my family, and others?"

Asking yourself these questions and acting upon your answers allows you to act with integrity. Integrity allows other people to trust you and get close to you. They know there will be no surprise resentments or passive-aggressiveness.

Growing up also allows you to discover your passions and energetically pursue them. People-pleasers spend a lot of time doing things for which they have no passion because they either never ask themselves what they want, or if they do ask themselves, they never get around to doing anything about it.

The ability to ask yourself what you want, take steps toward that goal and to then hold on to yourself when there is pressure to fuse (i.e., to give into others' wants due to your own anxiety) is one example of how relationships are such powerful crucibles for your own growth. When you ask yourself what you want and then do it—despite the anxiety from within or the resistance from without—you will grow and mature. Believe it or not, it is precisely this kind of growth and maturity that naturally attracts others to you and keeps them interested in you.

6. Growing the Authentic You requires you to fully love.
Your ability to love is directly related to your ability to tolerate your own anxiety. When someone you love triggers your anxiety—which will happen simply because they're in a relationship with you and the forces of togetherness and separateness are playing out—you will likely react in an attempt to change the anxiety within yourself. In other words, you'll often react because you want your spouse to change (rather than having to change yourself) so your anxiety will be relieved.

Intimacy triggers anxiety. For as many positive connotations that the word *intimacy* typically enjoys, intimacy is just as likely to be uncomfortable as it is to produce good feelings. So when you get closer to another person, your anxiety may also rise.

Remember Steve and Michelle's unfortunate vacation scenario? Michelle's lizard brain projects some imagined disaster on their upcoming vacation. If Steve is being authentic, he can see what is needed to give her space to move into her more authentic self as well.

There is no right way to deal with the situation. From a place of consciousness and being a hundred percent present, Steve's Authentic Self can be present in a way that allows Michelle to experience the natural process of change within the system of their marriage.

When she projects her anxieties about what might go wrong onto her spouse and tells him she can't trust him, Steve's Authentic Self could respond in a number of ways. He might playfully smile, pull her close, look into her eyes, and confidently state, "We're going to have an amazing time together on vacation."

Or he might say, "Let's sit down for a minute. Tell me what you're feeling anxious about." Steve will then listen without defending himself or trying to solve her problem and thereby gain a deeper understanding of what triggered her lizard brain. His calm presence might be enough to help her shift into her own place of authentic self-awareness.

Like gives way to like. In the same way that conflict tends to breed more conflict, love leads to love.

When you choose to take your Authentic Self down the path toward fully loving your spouse, he or she often intuitively understands that something significant has changed. Intrigued and attracted by this new you, they may want to follow in your footsteps.

But even if you learn how to live from your Authentic Self, even if you've pulled the curtain away from the person you've always tried to hide, your spouse may not respond in kind. But that should be OK with you. Having no attachment to outcome can sometimes mean facing hard truths within your relationship.

Appendix D: How to Self-Soothe

Self-soothing isn't changing something outside of you in order to lessen your anxiety. Rather, self-soothing is calming the anxiety within you as you continue to move forward in life. Sound too hard? Even infants learn how to do this. Here are more than a dozen ways to self-soothe.

Breathe
When stressed, your breathing becomes quick and shallow. Your shoulders hunch forward. When you're feeling stressed, breathe in deeply from your abdomen. Relax your shoulders. This changes the CO_2 level in your blood, slows your heartbeat, and relaxes your body and mind. Breathing is the most effective form of self-soothing.

Tell yourself: I can handle it
Most anxiety results from the false belief that you can't handle something. This could include whatever is happening around you in the present moment or whatever you're imagining is going to happen at some future time. Your mind convinces you that you can't handle things like rejection, someone being mad at you, looking foolish, being found out, being alone, or telling the truth. The next time you're conscious of feeling anxious, just repeat to yourself, "No matter what happens, I'll handle it." Continue to repeat that until your mind starts to believe it.

Remember gratitude
Much of our anxiety results from deprivation or scarcity thinking. Feeling grateful is very calming because it activates a different part of your brain. Consciously counting your blessings when you're feeling worried or anxious reminds you that you live in an abundant world. It also helps you to get out of your lizard brain and to attune yourself to a different part of your mind. Whenever you find yourself worrying or stressing about something, pause for a few moments and think about some of the things for which you are grateful. Maybe write these blessings down in a journal.

Shun niceness and perfectionism
Consciously let go of your need to be liked by everyone all the time and of your need to do everything perfectly. These are two of the biggest anxiety producers. Challenge the distorted beliefs that cause you to both seek approval and hide your mistakes.

Be in the moment
Unless someone is holding a loaded gun to your head or there's a man-eating tiger crouching next to you in the bushes, you really don't have much to be anxious about at this moment. For most of us, the world we live in isn't all that dangerous. And there are few real emergencies in our daily lives. Put simply, there aren't that many situations where we truly need to fight, run, or hide.

So, pause for a moment. Pay attention to your body and your immediate surroundings. Are you warm enough? Are you well fed? Are you in relatively good health? Are you safe? This is *The Now*. The present moment usually isn't all that bad. Dwelling in *The Now* helps soothe the anxiety your mind creates when it's focusing on some moment in the future.

Make an obsess appointment
If you have a worry spinning around in your brain, make an obsess appointment with yourself. Set aside ten minutes once a day and *consciously* obsess. Whenever you find yourself unconsciously obsessing throughout the day, tell your brain to stop. Limit all obsessing to your appointment time. Do this for three days, and you'll be amazed at the results.

Break it down
Break down whatever is making you anxious into little tasks. The anxious mind tends to make everything into a much bigger deal than it really is. No matter what's in front of you, you don't have to tackle the whole thing. Think of it this way: how do you eat an elephant? One bite at a time.

Take action
Thinking causes anxiety; acting cures it. One of the most powerful ways to soothe your anxiety is to forbid your mind from freaking itself out by over-thinking. Overcome the paralysis of analysis and take action. Do something — anything. If it turns out that your action wasn't the right choice, then learn from it and do something else. Overcome the tendency to sit and do nothing. If there is something you need to do, do it now. It doesn't become less stressful if you wait to do it later.

More self-soothing suggestions

- Talk to someone.
- Journal.
- Recall experiences when you successfully handled similar (or worse) situations.
- Visualize positive outcomes.
- Use humor.
- Meditate.
- Exercise.
- Practice yoga.
- Go for a walk.

Self-soothing is essential for maturity and growth. It empowers you to welcome and lean into challenges, change, adventure, and the unknown. It is also essential for acting with integrity.

Appendix E:
To-dos for great sex for women

Men and women are wired differently, so when it comes to the way each gender approaches life, distinctions abound. There's no place where this is more true than in the area of sex. Men often want steps to follow or procedures to accomplish. While women may like steps as well, I've found that most often women operate best with a to-do list.

Sex can be a delicate act that requires open and direct communication between two partners, yet a healthy sex life isn't just about communicating with your partner. You also need to make sure you're communicating honestly with yourself, which means listening to yourself.

✓ **To-Do #1: Clear your mind to be more present throughout your life, marriage, and sex.**

Visitors to Alaska's Denali National Park can only see its mountain peaks twenty to thirty days per year because the clouds there are so thick.

Twenty to thirty days a year! What if you took that trip? You save up money for the adventure of a lifetime—the opportunity to see, or even climb, the highest peak in North America. You travel thousands of miles to reach the beginning of the adventure only to discover that you cannot see where you're going. Clouds and weather force you to turn around.

Doesn't life sometimes feel this way? You can't see where you're going, and there are only a few mornings when you wake up and clearly know your path or purpose.

Clarity is the ability to see both near and far with accuracy, understanding, and insight. When you know where you want to go, and perhaps more importantly where you currently are, life becomes less complicated and circumstances are easier to navigate.

Think about the times in your life when you've been clear, when it felt like you were in the flow and had energy and a zest for life.

How do you find better clarity?

Start by clearly identifying your gifts. What are your particular strengths, abilities, skills, and attitudes? When you clearly know what you've been gifted with, you can choose how to use your gifts. Grab a notebook or piece of paper and name your gifts. Ask others for their input and see if you agree with their insights.

Society (and womanhood) seems to want you to be a Jill-of-all-trades. The problem is that often leaves you a master of nothing, which produces a mediocre relationship and life. You may be unsettled or bored and not know why. You may feel like you're spinning your wheels and getting nowhere fast. When you create clarity, you pick up momentum.

The next step for better clarity is write down what you want. Writing things down is a powerful tool in this process. Writing helps things become clear. Brainstorm the things you want in your life, marriage, and sex. Write it *all* down.

Wait a week, then go through your list and see what's realistic, accurate, and within your control. Work on one thing at a time. As you go through your days, notice your internal chatter. What do you tell yourself about what you want or are doing in the moment?

Along with your internal chatter, take note of your physical sensations: the butterflies in your stomach, times of shallow breathing or yawning, or stress carried in your shoulders or back. Work to become aware of the sensations you experience and your surroundings. Do this regularly, and you'll gain a clear picture of your life, which allows you to begin honing in on the more purposeful and meaningful actions you want to take.

An important side note: when you experience feelings of discomfort in this process (i.e., uneasiness, boredom, or agitation), it could be a signal that you've discovered a valuable area deserving of your focus. Growing up in life involves tolerating discomfort for the sake of growth. Stick with it. The reward on the other side will be worth it.

✓ To-Do #2: Allow yourself to be thought of (and think of yourself) as beautiful and loved.

Self-perception can lead to either confidence or doubt. You'd be surprised how often a woman will tell me her husband tells her he loves her and believes she's sexy, but she doesn't believe it herself.

As a woman, you may be pretty good at seeing your own flaws, but is your perception accurate?

The first step is to focus on yourself, which is often particularly difficult for women. It seems to go against your nurturing nature, but it's very important.

Life require space. When we don't have enough space, we're often reactive and playing catch-up all day long.

Imagine this scenario: you're standing in line at the store and you feel an impatient person right behind you. She's shifting back and forth, mumbling something inaudible under her breath while crowding your space, as if doing so will cause the line to move faster. If you move forward, you'll crowd the person in front of you. You're stuck.

What feelings do you associate with this scenario?

Now imagine that you're having sex with your husband and he's only going through the motions—or you are. No connection exists other than the physical. Your mind is littered with the tasks of the day, the fantasy of better times, or even someone else.

What feelings do you associate with this experience?

Without space you are unable to be fully present. You simply have no room, so the important things in your life are shoved to the back of the line in order to address what's immediate.

✓ **To-Do #3: Before any sexual interaction, consciously ask yourself if you truly feel like having sex, which sexual behaviors you feel like performing, and which you don't.**

Far too often women end up having sex when they don't want to. The most common reason why people repeatedly engage in mediocre sex (at best) is to avoid an argument with their spouse. The problem is that obligatory sex is never truly satisfying and often leads to shameful feelings that you hold your spouse responsible for.

Oftentimes sex becomes routine and burdensome because there's not enough space in your head, in your schedule, or in your emotions. Learning how to carve out space for yourself and your husband requires you to make yourself and your needs, wants, and desires a priority.

Because space is such a nebulous word, let's consider these five areas of space:

Physical space allows for comfort. When things are in place, there is a flow to getting things done. Physical space is the shared space in your relationship. Remember, you share your life with another human being by choice. You share a house, a room, a bathroom, and a closet.

How do these spaces look right now? What do you suppose would happen if you made your master bedroom more of a romantic haven? Spend time this week and declutter your room.

My personal recommendation is that **the bedroom ought to be reserved for two things: sleep and sex.**

Get rid of the piles of stuff—the laundry, the TV, the computers, etc.—and make it a peaceful getaway. Also, take all the "business" conversations outside of the bedroom. Pay bills elsewhere. Have tense conversations somewhere else. Reserve your bedroom for *only* sleep and sex. You'll see a difference in your relationship.

Mental space allows you to be present in the moment and provides you with space to create, reminisce, honor, cherish, and love. When mental space isn't present, busyness takes over.

Too little mental space leads to lying in bed at night unable to sleep because your mind is racing, which leads to being unable to really connect with your husband because you have no room in your head (or he can't possibly keep up with the speed of your thoughts).

You can begin clearing your mental space by looking at what's bugging you: unfinished projects, clutter, unresolved issues, housework, just getting by, etc. Address what you can: the things *you* are responsible for. Confront yourself about whether the things you want to do are the things you really should do or even want to do. The key is to be specific, honest, and accurate.

Consider this statement: *"I don't like sex."* When it comes to confronting your sex life honestly, this may be a true and acceptable start, but it's too broad and open for inaccuracy. This statement may put you in the ballpark, but a more specific, accurate statement could be:

"I am so preoccupied and busy with work and other things that I spend little quality time with my husband. In fact, I come home every night and obsess about work, so I can't unwind."

Other explanations could include past trauma or guilt associated with sex. This is a more accurate assessment of a situation because the problem is outlined in more detail. With such a concrete self-assessment, it's easier to find solutions to the problems in your sex life.

The space of time provides the opportunity for you to accomplish what's important to you. With enough time, life is clear and purposeful. But when there isn't enough time, you feel rushed and frazzled. It's easy to have low to no standards for how to use your time, which reveals poor boundaries. Then you waste time by only handling the immediate and rarely returning to the important.

So ask yourself:

- How much time do I have for myself?
- How much time do I have for my relationship?
- Am I using my time well?

When you understand the role time plays in your relationship, you have the power to choose how to spend that time. If you don't allow margins in your life for time, your relationship and sex life will deteriorate.

Emotional space allows you to experience the whole range of life's emotions. When you have emotional room, you can listen to your emotions with less risk of being dominated by them. You can be close to others without fear of being lost or smothered.

Every one of us has certain amounts of emotional clutter, and especially in the area of sex, like past issues, hurts, grief, and grudges. Just like the stacks of clutter in your office or home, it's beneficial to **clear away emotional clutter.** Seek help through counseling, hire a professional coach, or take a vacation. When you create more emotional space, you'll experience more out of life.

Spiritual space that is open and clear allows your gifts and talents to be evident and free- flowing. When your spiritual space is cramped or blocked, you lose access to intuition and your deeper self.

So much of your learning comes from internal listening, or your intuition. **Pray, meditate, read spiritual writings, or listen to uplifting music.** Connecting with God pulls you out of yourself. It helps to keep things in perspective, gives you hope, and expands your ability to enjoy more in life. It calls you up into a story bigger than yourself.

Have you ever prayed or connected to your spiritual nature regarding sex? Try it. Seek the spiritual side of sex. Seek the sacredness of sex. Pray before, during and after. It's a beautiful and God-designed thing. Embrace it.

✓ To-Do #4: Be flexible about the length of the sexual interaction.

This may surprise you, but many people would have sex more often with their spouses if they didn't feel that the sexual interaction didn't have to be such a time-consuming interaction. Let's face it: most everyone is busy and overloaded with to-dos. But the truth is that a sexual interaction doesn't need to be a long, drawn-out event.

The point is to **be flexible and to check-in with your spouse before the interaction.** Ask, "Do you feel like trying [insert behavior] tonight, or do you just want to [insert behavior]?" Asking such questions shows that you're flexible and open to simply being together sexually rather than walking into the interaction and thinking that you'll only feel satisfied if the interaction meets certain prescribed criteria.

✓ To-Do #5: Accept the fact that orgasm isn't necessary for the sexual experience to be considered a good one.

Having an orgasm isn't the only thing that defines a sexual experience, though some people (millions upon millions) struggle with this idea. The danger of putting such a strict condition on sex is that it causes the sex to turn into a competitive event or a goal to be reached every time, usually at the expense of real intimacy. **The goals ought to be openness to orgasms if the mood and timing are right and to approach sex as a natural, go-with-the-flow experience.**

✓ To-Do #6: Realize you have more control over your sex life than you think.

Learning to be more conscious and engaged through life and sex requires you taking on you. The quality (and quantity) begins and ends with you.

Others will have influence over what happens, but you are the major player in the creation of the life you desire. You are the star of your story.

Learning to be more conscious is an art that involves incorporating some of your own desires, goals, and dreams, and being aware of yourself and others in every moment. Every day brings you face-to-face with the give-and-take of marriage. Blindly seeking your own desires and goals will likely cause you to hurt not only yourself but those you care about. You can, however, begin sharing your dreams and desires with your spouse and listen to their dreams and desires too.

Actually, many of these to-dos are interconnected. When you work on one, you're working on the others too.

Now go check off some to-dos.

Appendix F:
Three rules for great sex

Dr. Robert Glover, a colleague and mentor of mine, suggests these "rules" to help you experience a better sex life with your spouse. They're targeted toward men (as I believe men prefer to lead in the bedroom and women want to be led in the bedroom), but they can easily be applied to both sexes. As you read these rules, give careful consideration to whether or not this is how you approach sex or if you can begin to integrate these rules into your sex life. I'm willing to bet that once you do that, you'll start to have fulfilling and intimate moments with your spouse that you may have thought would never happen.

- Approach your wife as if she is the most adventurous, passionate, and open-minded woman in the world. When you assume less than this, you limit the possibilities of excitement in the relationship.
- It's her job to say no to anything she's not interested in trying or doing. It's your job to speak up and express your desires.
- Don't take things personally. If she says no to sex on the roof tonight, don't take it personally, then refer back to Rule 1.

Let's look at each of these rules in-depth.

Rule 1: Approach optimistically

Approach your spouse with the assumption that she will like everything you do to her and with her. This is your job. Most men violate this rule in two significant ways:

- Husbands approach their wives passively, try to please them, and attempt to avoid rejection at all costs.
- Husbands wait for their wives to initiate sex so they, as men, can feel desired and wanted.

Many men who are frustrated about their sexual relationships with their spouses are passive, timid lovers. They don't want to offend their wives or do anything that will make her think badly of them. They get attached to outcome and try to please her so she'll want to have sex again in the near future.

What they fail to realize is that their passivity and anxiety dim any fire of desire in their spouses. What's appealing and attractive about a man who lacks confidence in the one area where he should exude confidence?

Such passivity also forces the wife to be the gatekeeper of sex. It also puts the responsibility on her to manage her husband's feelings and insecurities. Because the gatekeeper has the keys that can allow or prevent entry, the gatekeeper holds all the power. And neither spouse should have all the power in a relationship.

A sexually insecure and passive man tends to blame his wife for her sexual unavailability or seeming lack of interest in sex. As resentment builds, he often falls into a pattern of emotional eruptions, passive-aggressiveness, and not-so-subtle manipulation. The more the man follows this approach, the more his wife loses interest in being sexual with him. The more she loses interest, the more resentment builds. Because of this seemingly unending cycle of cold shoulders and resentment, sex eventually becomes a long-forgotten, hoped-for experience within the marriage—which can then lead to either spouse seeking to get his or her sexual needs met elsewhere.

While we're on that topic, let's quickly discuss why you *shouldn't* be sexual outside of your marriage. There's more to monogamy than the fact that it's one of the Ten Commandments. Furthermore, true monogamy is an inner manifestation, not an outer legislation.

Keep all of your sexual energy in the relationship. It's one of the most powerful ways to deepen your marriage and keep your love life simmering so that it can quickly boil when necessary. Plus, for the men, consciously focusing all of your sexual desire and expression exclusively toward your woman is one of the most powerful and attractive things a man can do.

Many people have a pretty loose definition of fidelity, so let's define it better. Being faithful to your spouse means you don't do anything with another person that you wouldn't do with your own sibling. It means not doing anything with another person that you wouldn't do if your spouse were standing right next to you. Fidelity is not the opposite of infidelity. Fidelity isn't what you don't do, what you don't get caught doing, or what you wish you could do but choose not to. *Fidelity is showing up, with all of yourself, for your spouse.*

The first way to keep all of your sexual energy in your relationship is to stop masturbating. If you relieve sexual tension through masturbation, you rob yourself of a life force that is meant to drive you to your spouse. This also means completely cutting out porn. Pornography conditions men to have impersonal, goal-oriented, performance sex.

These distorted images and behaviors often get transferred to a personal sexual relationship.

The same boundaries apply to sexual fantasies. Use those fantasies to connect with your spouse, not to separate yourself from her. Stop thinking about some other person's body while you're with your spouse. Your spouse (especially the wives) will sense your lack of presence and put emotional walls up without even being aware of it or knowing why. The only time any of the above practices are appropriate is when they're shared in the marriage relationship together. Show up and share all of yourself with your spouse. That's the most loving gift you can give.

Some men use the excuse of a sexless marriage to indulge themselves in sexual practices outside of marriage and then blame their wives for their own actions. They admit something many men in my office often do: "I just wish my wife would initiate sex more often." Some men (who don't know any better but should) go so far as to hold back and wait for their wives to take the lead. This is a test she is bound to fail, thus further reinforcing the man's insecurities and resentment.

Hear this: *Women aren't wired to initiate sex. They are wired to be receptive.*

This isn't to say women don't like sex—most do. What I'm saying is that they aren't wired by Mother Nature to initiate sex. To be blunt, women are designed to be penetrated. If a woman doesn't seem to like sex, it's usually due to one of two reasons: she has either been sexually violated at some time in her life or she is with a man who doesn't know how to handle her well. That's harsh, but true.

Not only are women *not wired* to be the sexual aggressors, they are turned off by an insecure, anxious man. When a woman turns down the needy approach of an insecure man, it may feel like she is rejecting sex, but she isn't. A healthy woman wants to be penetrated by a confident man, not manipulated by an insecure little boy.

To be that confident man, approach your wife as if she has always said yes to *every one* of your advances. This rule isn't about sexual technique; it's about you not censoring yourself or holding back in any way. It's about you being a complete and whole man and letting her experience all of you. In other words, approach her like you did early in the marriage when you were pretty sure she wanted sex as much as you did. Approach her like she's a freak and will love everything you do to her.

In order to accomplish this, you must let go of your expectations in regard to how your spouse will respond. In fact, sex is great practice for letting go. If you stop trying to assume what she wants (or what will make her give you what you want), you can take all kinds of chances. As soon as you start assuming, you become passive and will struggle with taking a chance or putting yourself out there, sexually speaking.

When you approach your wife "as if" *and* she trusts you, she will let go and let you take her. The very act of trusting you enough to take her beyond her comfort zone, knowing that you would never do anything that would harm her, builds more trust and makes her feel secure in ways that nothing else can—which intensifies her trust and her willingness to let go even more in the future.

Rule 2: Don't assume her no
Your wife should be able to say no to *anything* she's not interested in trying or doing when it comes to naked playtime. However, *you* should be able to confidently speak up and clearly express your desires when it comes to sex.

This yes/no dynamic is essential in order for you to be able to approach her as if she is profoundly into you (which we've learned by now is a natural turn-on to a vast majority of guys). If you know that she has no qualms about letting you know what she doesn't like or when she's not interested in having sex, you don't have to figure anything out about her or hold back in any way when it comes to what you *will* do when she's ready to roll around with you.

Don't make the job of sex the hardest part of your night. Trust that your mature spouse will likewise confidently speak her mind and tell you no when she needs to. Don't assume her no for her; assume yes and allow her to make her own decision. Again, this is a prime example of where having little to no attachment to the outcome of your request helps grow you as a person.

When you automatically assume her no, you're essentially trying to read her mind. First, no one can do that. Second, that game typically results in making you timid and tentative in approaching your wife for sex. You might as well start talking about dividends and capital gains for that is as attractive as an unconfident man is in bed. Much more often than not, this approach sets you up for failure. At best, it engenders a sex life characterized by boring and infrequent sex. (And no truly great stories suffer a romantic subplot like that!)

When you trust her to say no if she wants to but assume her yes, that allows you the freedom to pursue your wildest dreams. You can boldly set the tone and take the lead. Thought and desire give way to instinct and (healthy) lust. Sex becomes adventuresome and not just something the two of you do in order to fulfill selfish desires.

In a way, sex is the ultimate manifestation of differentiation: you have sex because of the intense pleasure it brings you, but in the same moment you're providing intense pleasure to your spouse. You're simultaneously giving to get and getting to give. Sex is selfish *and* self-giving. Either motivation by itself could be considered wrong, but when working in tandem—when sex is pursued both for what it gives to you and for what you can give to your spouse through it—sex is otherworldly.

When two emotionally mature people who trust each other engage in adventurous sex, well, no is a word you'll rarely hear.

Rule 3: Don't allow her no to become personal
You will hear no from time to time. It's likely you've already heard it, and maybe far too often. Maybe you've heard it so often that you've give up even trying to get a yes. You've found yourself in an unending cycle you don't know how to free yourself from. This rule is for you.

When you receive a no to a sexual advance on your wife, don't take it personally. Again, don't assume anything about your wife's motivation for saying no. Don't automatically assume any number of things that us men are so prone to assume in the face of a no:

- I did something wrong.
- I'm a bad man/husband/dad.
- She didn't like it last time.
- She doesn't like when I try new things.
- She never wants to have sex again.
- She's seeing someone else.

Don't play this losing game. Tell yourself that her no simply means no, then go back to Rule #1: Approach optimistically. Don't have a shame attack or withdraw. Don't lose your "phallic-ness" or your erection. Don't roll over and pout and make her rescue you. Stay in your masculinity. Start over with Rule #1 and continue approaching her as if she wants everything you want to give her.

How you handle when she says no affects her ability to feel aroused by you. If you pout, she'll feel like the most powerful person in the room—which will kill her desire for sex with you. If you handle it well, it will make you look confident and deepen her trust in you, thus arousing her. Remember, she wants to be penetrated by you, not take care of your fragile feelings.

If you decide to try something new while making love and your spouse says no, hold on to yourself (well, don't literally hold on to yourself. That'd likely create more problems.) Her no doesn't mean you did something wrong or that she thinks you're perverted for wanting to do *that*. Her no may not even mean she never wants you to do that again. Remember: don't assume anything! Soothe yourself and stay present. In time, consider discussing her refusal so that you know what to try next time. And be sure there's a next time quite soon. That will display your confidence and show her that you're not withdrawing or pouting because you didn't get what you wanted.

Frank and graphic talk for men
Until now, I've held back on what I think most men need to hear. If you're ready to be challenged, if you're ready for your sex life to be what you've always imagined, read on. Consider this fair warning.

Sex talks with clients in my office are always interesting. Though some are reticent to share the intimate details of their sex lives, many open up after a little prodding. I recall a married couple in particular where I had an inclination that the husband was timid, nice guy intent on always pleasing his wife and ensuring she was happy. So I asked him a hard question:

"Have you ever had a time when you really took your wife sexually?"

His wife answered before he did, and even before she spoke, I already knew what the answer was going to be. After all, *she* was the one speaking on his behalf.

"No! I don't think he's actually man enough to do something like that!"

For a moment, let's put the unfortunate relationship dynamics that his wife's response revealed on hold. To be blunt, the problem was that the man was living his life without his penis screwed on tightly. Men need to embrace their healthy masculine power so that women can then live out their femininity and its power within them.

Most women find these rules for great sex liberating. They're also more receptive to these rules than most men. Women like that the burden is taken off of them to make sex happen. They also like knowing that they can say no anytime, which makes it *easier* for them to say yes more often. Plus, women like knowing they won't be burdened by an insecure man's emotions when they say no. They can speak their mind to a strong man.

Men often spend a lot of time indirectly trying to get their women in the mood for sex. I suggest that you *never* try to get an unaroused woman aroused. It's a powerful mistake that leads to all sorts of hurt feelings, unmet expectations, and more. Pushing your wife to have sex isn't sexy, and especially with her biology, such pressure isn't any good for her physically, which is why foreplay is so important. Your wife needs time to heat up, and with heating up, her body naturally responds and gets ready to receive you.

As a man, it's your job to set the tone and take the lead. When men follow these rules, it deepens their wives' trust in them. Every time a man approaches his wife as if she'll say yes, and she trusts him enough to let go, she experiences one of the deepest emotional experiences a woman can know. The process of letting go is what opens her up (and she can't do it for herself, by the way). The greatest gift you can give your wife is the opportunity to experience the depth of her feminine essence. And when she experiences that, you get to experience it as well.

Getting Personal
You're not alone in being confused about what you should do, or why your wife is acting *that* way, when it comes to your sex life. I often experienced anxiety when my wife was sexually assertive, regardless of how subtle or obvious her overtures were. And for a long time I didn't understand my lizard-brain reaction. Shouldn't I *want* her to want me like that? Shouldn't I count my lucky stars that she would come after me from time to time? I like sex as much as the next guy, but her advances made me nervous. Sometimes I would even shut down and find ways to avoid sex. Ultimately, this confused me and frustrated my wife.

But a different perspective on what was occurring helped me realize my role in those moments. Though this may sound strange to some, stick with me. When my wife communicated her sexual desire for me, she was behaving with masculine energy. Because she was essentially telling me what to do (even subtly) and I sought to acquiesce, I behaved with feminine energy—and this is OK. Despite my long discussions on the importance of living through your masculinity, marriage relationships are a constant back and forth flow of masculine and feminine energy. Though men shouldn't persistently live with a feminine mindset, choosing to allow your wife to have control from time to time is healthy and can add an adventuresome dimension to your sex life.

If your spouse is penetrating you with her sexual desire (masculine), and you are the receiver of that penetration (feminine), you don't have to try to penetrate her (masculine) from a receptive position (feminine). When you're aware of this, you have two options: consciously "out-masculine" her by upping the ante and penetrating her (emotionally and physically) in a dominant way, or consciously stay in the feminine and allow her to penetrate you.

Sex is a great way to practice letting the woman climb into the driver's seat (so to speak) for a little while. If you're already setting the tone and taking the lead, it frees her up to throw you down, climb on, and ride for a while! Sex is also a great place to practice the back and forth of dominating and submitting—a metaphor for how your relationship ought to work in general.

Such reciprocity can only happen if the man leads from the beginning. Once the woman trusts that her man is willing to set the tone, she can occasionally take the lead and then hand it back again. The woman can reverse the rules and apply them just as the man does. But she will only feel free to do so if she knows she won't have to *stay* in the driver's seat. When a couple develops this kind of back and forth— penetrating and receiving—the sex and the relationship get really interesting!

This allows for elegant reciprocity in the sexual relationship. It also offers both of you an opportunity to experiment with sexual polarity as you consciously move in and out of your masculine and feminine. But most significantly, this awareness can help you soothe your anxiety and let go of any performance expectation.

Bonus Rule #4: If she can make it hard, it's hers.
Speaking of letting go of performance expectation, what if this rule was often followed in your house? Guys, would you agree to this rule? (I'm not sure *any* guy with his libido still intact would refuse.) From what I can tell with my clients, I'm pretty sure the wives enjoy this rule as much as the husbands.

Women like it because they don't have to wait for their man to get into the mood to penetrate them. Men appreciate it because it takes the pressure off of them to always be the penetrator, especially when they're busy, distracted, tired, or in an emotionally receptive place.

If a wife has permission to use her feminine skills to get her man aroused (with no attachment to outcome), and the man is not obligated to respond in any way, some interesting things can happen. Rule #4 also adds two powerful components to a dynamic sexual relationship: it allows the man to stay more present and increases the odds of the woman getting what she wants.

Everybody wins!

Final Thoughts on Better Sex
A word of caution, guys: these rules for sex are *extremely* powerful.

Your wife will love them, and the results will scare you to death—which is why many men conveniently forget them. But these rules can cause your spouse to emotionally attach to you in a profound way. She will desire to be opened by you with regularity. She may even want to fuse and meld with you in an unhealthy manner, and this is where your practice in differentiating and self-soothing will be essential. Your first impulse might be to push back or run away when she wants to fuse. Hold on to yourself. Keep being present with her, but keep your boundaries clear, and remember to honor the other aspects of your life as well.

In other words, remember to write a great story with your life, one that includes romance and adventure and a quest for fulfillment. Don't rely on any one person, event, title, failure, or achievement to define who you are. Rather, shed every fig-leaf lie you've ever used to hide yourself from being truly known.

Then you'll learn what it means to enjoy a truly naked marriage!

Printed in Great Britain
by Amazon